The Exquisite Table

A History of French Cuisine

by
Esther B. Aresty

The Bobbs-Merrill Company, Inc.
Indianapolis/New York

Also by Esther B. Aresty

The Delectable Past
The Best Behavior
The Grand Venture

Copyright © 1980 by Esther B. Aresty

All rights reserved, including the right of reproduction
in whole or in part in any form
Published by the Bobbs-Merrill Company, Inc.
Indianapolis   New York

Designed by Marcia Ben-Eli
Manufactured in the United States of America

First printing

Library of Congress Cataloging in Publication Data

Aresty, Esther B
  The exquisite table.

  1.Cookery, French—History.   I.Title
TX719.A714   641.5'944'09   79-55441
ISBN 0-672-52307-8

To the memory of Evelyn Gendel

Acknowledgments

My grateful thanks to Pierre Escoffier for the use of his grandfather's personal papers and notes, and for his gracious help.

Thanks also to M. Rameau, director of the *Musée d'Escoffier* in Villeneuve-Loubet, France, for giving me access to the *Musée*'s archives. And to Nicole Villa at the Bureau d'Estampes of the Bibliotheque Nationale in Paris (now at the Musée de Louvre), my thanks for her helpful advice.

Contents

The Age of Carême

The Age of Escoffier

Introduction

I n France everything that is art is pervaded by the gallic spirit. It has homogenized a diverse people into a nation with an instinct for what is tasteful and elegant, and in no French art is this more vigorously asserted than in the art of cooking.

Since the cuisine first took shape in the seventeenth century, at a time that coincided with the rise of France as the dominant political and cultural force in western Europe, it has been the leader in the western world. It has remained the leader, unaffected by the ups and downs of its nation's fortunes.

Like any country with different people and regions, France has more than one cuisine. Each is a story in itself. But the most familiar—what usually comes to mind as French—is the cuisine practiced by professional chefs, known variously as *haute, grande,* and classic. Within it lies the core of all French cooking, regardless of regional variations.

French willingness to absorb new ideas, and to adopt and adapt what was excellent elsewhere, constantly expanded the cuisine. New dishes were added like so much vocabulary. The cuisine became an international culinary language, yet retained its distinctive gallic quality.

Three stages marked this evolution. Many talented chefs contributed, but three were the principal architects: La Varenne, Carême, and Escoffier. Each chef combined great artistic talent with the skills of organization and communication, and each made his methods known in books that others could follow.

The Germans, Italians, Spaniards, and English made statements about their national cuisines as soon as printed books began to appear. All were on record by the end of the sixteenth century. Not the French—not until 1651, when François Pierre La Varenne organized their cuisine into *Le Vrai Cuisinier François* (The True French Cook). La Varenne was the first to give the cuisine form.

It was at once apparent that French cuisine was lighter and more delicate than the others. But like all cuisines at the time it was fairly simple, bound by cooking methods that had scarcely changed since medieval days. Oven heat was haphazard; ovens were heated by whatever fuel was available and the coals were withdrawn when the food went in. Surface cookery was equally uncertain. The spit and the fireplace ruled cookery in homes of all classes.

The cuisine took its cue chiefly from royalty and the nobility. The various cookery manuals that appeared were meant for the chefs in these seigneurial households, but the cooks and maid servants of the lesser bourgeoisie also consulted them. Frenchmen at all economic levels esteemed a good table and ate as well as their circumstances permitted. The cuisine expanded perceptibly during the reign of Louis XV, but did not approach the extravagant breadth and richness of the *grande cuisine* until the *ancien regime* ended in 1793. This first period may rightly be called the age of La Varenne.

With the Revolution, a new privileged class arose. New titles were minted by Napoleon and new nobles created right and left among the bourgeoisie. Their hunger for a grand table matched that of any old-line prince; if anything, the newcomers wanted it grander. So did the rulers of petty kingdoms and dukedoms, yearning to create a semblance of a brilliant French court in their small territories.

Chefs prepared more elaborate dishes than ever before. As the Industrial Revolution brought controlled heat for ovens, the art of the pastry maker expanded and brought fame to Antonin Carême, a pastry chef whose talent for the grandiose and spectacular was so great that the future George IV of England and the Emperor Alexander of Russia begged for his services.

At this point French cuisine divided. The preparation of *grande* dishes now demanded too much time and skill to be adaptable to the bourgeois kitchen. Furthermore, there seemed to be many strange *new* dishes. But Antoine Beauvilliers, a chef turned restaurateur, contended that they were the same old dishes covered over with new sauces, forcemeats, bristling *hatelets* (ornamental skewers) and *names—à la the duc de this* and *à la the comte de that,* according to the fancy of the chefs who served these personages. Beauvilliers set matters straight for average cooks in a two-volume work that contained the established classics of French cuisine under their straightforward names.

At the same time Carême began a similar undertaking for *grande* kitchens. He included most of the standard dishes but made even the simplest seem complicated, treating the *pot-au-feu* to four pages of analysis.

The bulk of Carême's work dealt with the newcomers to the cuisine, basic dishes now garnished and decorated beyond recognition. Carême had learned some of these new variations from his revered teachers Avise and Laguipierre, noted chefs of the Napoleonic period, but many were his own invention. He included Russian and Polish specialties that had won his favor during his stints for princes of these nations. He gave special attention and space to sauces, which now numbered more than two hundred. One volume dealt only with *pièces montées,* decorative creations of pastry and marzi-

pan that demonstrated the skill of the pastry chef; they were made in such shapes as oriental temples, crenellated castles, even cascading waterfalls. Without a *pièce montée* at its center a *grande* table was virtually bare.

Carême devoted almost half of his forty-nine years to the task he had set himself, which finally ran to twelve volumes solely for "the homes of the *grandes*." When the work was completed Carême had fathered the *grande* or *haute* cuisine of France. He died in 1833 and was succeeded in eminence and surpassed in ostentation by Urbain Dubois, chef to the king of Prussia.

Dubois exerted little influence on the cuisine itself, though he did bring in additional foreign dishes. However, he helped to modernize table service, doing away with the placement of all the food on the table at one time to grow cold as the meal progressed. Instead, he favored serving a course at a time. He was also an advocate of eating with the fork in the left hand, not then a universal custom in France. Dubois composed several large and exceedingly heavy books which helped to perpetuate the age of Carême.

The mode of life changed as industry and commerce became dominant. Railroads spread. All classes traveled. Hotels and restaurants came to the fore. Many of the most accomplished chefs now catered to public taste, pleasing not an employer but a multitude of patrons. It was no longer a competition of hosts vying to set the finest table, but of restaurants contending for these patrons in the hope that their praise would bring in other diners.

The *grande cuisine* was now practiced in the kitchens of the better-class restaurants, but for many chefs, and for diners as well, it was *too* grand, too labored, too reminiscent of vanished times and unsuitable to the fast-approaching twentieth century. It needed to be modernized, simplified, reshaped to please the many rather than the few. A new leader emerged who had spent his entire professional life in restaurants serving the public. The cuisine entered a new phase which, in some ways, seemed closer to its beginnings. We shall call this the age of Escoffier and begin our story.

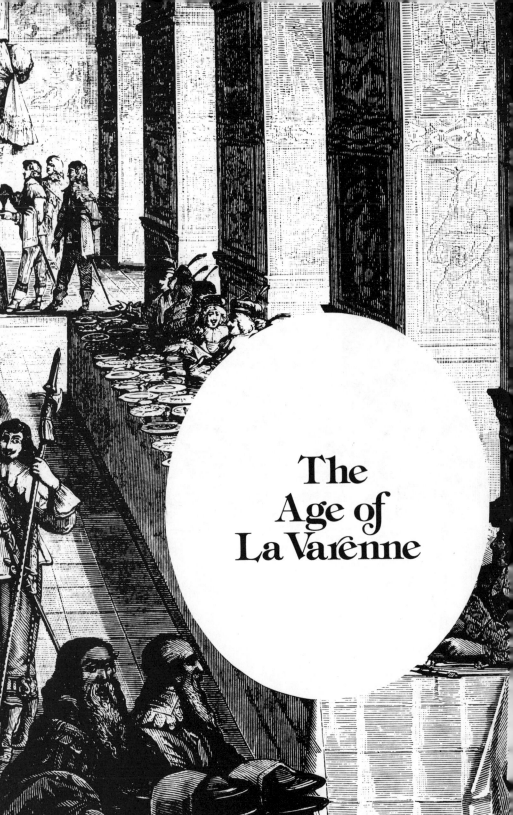

The
Age of
La Varenne

CUISINIER FRANCOIS

The True
French Cook
Dispels a Myth

"The psychology of a country finds expression chiefly in its cooking."
Alain Laubreaux

When it comes to cooking with grace, subtlety, and just plain talent, everybody seems to agree that the French score the highest. Why, then, is it commonly accepted, even by many of the French, that they were taught this art by the Italians? It seems to be a case of the emperor's clothes. If everybody says so, it must be so.

If the various claims to support this belief are examined carefully, the whole idea appears to be based on myth. When, where, and how it began is uncertain. It usually centers on Catherine de Medici bringing cooks to the court of France, though Marie de Medici, a later queen of France, occasionally comes in for a share of credit.

"Cookery received its impetus in France with the advent of Catherine de Medici at the court of Francis I . . . bringing her cooks with her from her native country," Charles Ellwanger writes in *Pleasures of the Table.* "It was under Henry III [Catherine's son], about 1580, that the delicacies of the Italian

3

table were introduced at Paris," according to A. V. Kirwan in *Host and Guest*.

One can almost hear the blare of trumpets as Christian Guy, a French writer of more recent date, makes his proclamation. "One of the greatest dates in the history of French cooking . . . is October 20, 1553 . . . when Catherine de Medici was married to the future Henry II . . . the Italian Renaissance had at last succeeded in infiltrating France . . . the princess, followed by . . . a battalion of cooks, was to turn the world topsy-turvy . . . a Renaissance of the table was ushered in amid a riot of luxury."

One statement is true in all the foregoing. Catherine came to the court of Francis I to marry the future Henry II of France. The correct date was 1533.

Catherine, fourteen at the time, was accompanied by twelve young ladies-in-waiting near her own age, and, undoubtedly, a large retinue that included cooks and servants to wait on the large party that brought her by ship to Marseilles and cared for the travelers on the overland voyage to the French court. But as for installing cooks at the court of Francis I to serve her own needs—that would have been bringing coals to Newcastle, and unthinkable in any case with a monarch like Francis I. At that time his court was far more elegant than any court in Italy. "The foremost court in Europe," is how the historian Jean Heritier described it.

Furthermore, such an idea would never had occured to the unassuming, undemanding young girl, described by the Venetian ambassador as *molto obediente*—never mind that forty years later she gave the nod to the massacre of St. Bartholomew's Eve. In 1533 her chief desire was to please her new father-in-law, with whom she had already established a warm relationship through correspondence, and to become completely French as soon as possible.

She was already half French through her mother, Madeleine de la Tour d'Auvergne, who died at her birth. That French blood was her saving grace in the eyes of some French who frowned on the Medicis' bourgeois origin, though Catherine's uncle, Giovanni de Medici, had elevated the family rank when he became Pope Leo X. Had that not been the case, the gifts that Catherine brought along for her new relatives would have been presented without ceremony because "kings did not accept gifts from tradespeople in public." So much for the Medicis.

Another so-called proof offered in support of Italian culinary influence at the French court comes via Michel de Montaigne, the French essayist and philosopher, who was prominent at court late in Catherine's reign as queen of France. Montaigne is often quoted as praising Italian cooks at Catherine's court. Actually he was joking when he described an encounter with such a cook, "late in the kitchen of Cardinal Caraffia," and spoke of that cook's "magisterial gravity" when discussing his art, "the weighty and important considerations . . . [in] lofty, magnificent words, the very same we use when we discourse upon the government of an Empire."

The encounter did not take place at the court but while Montaigne was interviewing the cook as a prospective employee. The conversation struck Montaigne as so hilarious that he was inspired to write an essay on "how to make little things appear big." He called it *On the Vanity of Words.* William Hazlitt, editor of the nineteenth-century edition of Montaigne's essays, called the passage, "The palate-science pleasantly ridiculed."

Montaigne found little to praise in Italian cooking when he traveled in Italy in 1570. "Provisions are not half so plentiful . . . and not near so well [prepared]," he reported. He gave the nod to Venice for the best cooking and completely ignored the cuisine of Florence, summing up that Medici stronghold as "the most expensive city in Italy."

As for the Italian Renaissance at last "infiltrating France" with Catherine's arrival—a French Renaissance had been in stride since the fifteenth century. True, the seeds had wafted over from Italy into France, as they had into other countries, but wherever the Renaissance took root, what matured from the semination emerged differently in each country—on canvases, in books, and in architecture.

Woodcut showing 15th century diners at table.

National cuisines were a different matter. They developed over centuries, determined by climate, regional characteristics, quality of soil, and what the land was able to produce as a result of these factors. Poor pasturage for grazing, counterbalanced by plentiful olive trees, produced an oil-based cuisine in Italy. Verdant meadows made butter and cream abundant in France and the basis of its early cuisine. French cuisine had been growing in its own national direction long before Catherine de Medici came to France, and was as fully formed by 1533 as cookery and dining then allowed. At best, all national cuisines were still medieval. Forks were not yet in general use. Spoon and finger foods were the rule: hashes, stews, potages, and meats sliced thin enough to be speared on the point of a knife to be eaten by hand, or laid on a slice of bread and swallowed in a few gulps.

Nor did Marie de Medici, who came to the French court in 1600 as the second wife of Henry IV, have any pronounced effect on the cuisine. Any Italian touches she introduced were

Machiavellian rather than gastronomical. Her instinct for political meddling was acute, but from what can be gathered in accounts of court life at the time, she did little to advance taste or elegance at Henry's folksy, almost crude court. That came about during the reign of Louis XIII, the son Marie bore Henry, a reign which might more rightly be called the reign of Richelieu.

Richelieu! Now there was a man with polished taste. He restored majesty and refinement to the court and is said to have introduced many refinements to the table as well, including knives with rounded ends. The sight of diners picking their teeth with the sharply pointed knives then in use revolted him. He is also credited with sponsoring a plate deep enough to hold broth along with the solid elements of a potage, for reasons made clear in this passage from *Les Délices de la Campagne,* a book for affluent bourgeois households:

"Guests' plates should be deep, so that they can use them for soup . . . without taking it spoonful by spoonful out of the serving dish, as other guests might be disgusted at the sight of a spoon which has been in the mouth of a person, being dipped in the serving dish . . ."

When Richelieu died in 1642, he was succeeded by Mazarin, whose princely taste exceeded even Richelieu's and whose Italian cunning matched that of Marie de Medici. Italian though he was, born a Sicilian and the son of a groom at that, Mazarin thought of himself as a Frenchman and settled the matter by becoming a French citizen. His hand in guiding the affairs of France may have contributed to the notion of Italian influence in other areas, which was indeed apparent in earlier artistic developments under Francis I— Fontainebleau's Italianate landscaping, and its decorations by Italian painters headed by Da Vinci, who remained in France to live out his life as court painter to Francis I. But no marked Italian influence could be discerned in the cuisine of France when it was finally unveiled in 1651.

That year the first truly French cookbook appeared, and as if to say, "Let there be no mistake about how we French cook," it called itself *Le Vrai Cuisinier François* (The True

7

French Cook). Its author, François Pierre La Varenne, was chef to the Marquis d'Uxelles, a member of France's ancient nobility.

It was a tardy entry into the cookbook field. The Germans, English, and Italians had been producing printed cookbooks for almost a century, and the Italians had already established a claim to culinary leadership by producing the first one in 1475. The gallic quality of *Le Vrai Cuisinier François* was evident at once. It said nearly everything there was to say about French cuisine at the time and quickly became the voice of the French kitchen. Translated into English in 1653, it brought a flurry of English cooks to France to learn French ways and, in turn, to produce their own versions of French cooking.

One need only compare *Le Vrai Cuisinier François* to the cookbook by Bartolomeo Scappi, *Cooking Secrets of Pope Pius V*, at that time still the definitive work on Italian cooking, to see that no debt was owed to the Italians. Not that Italian cooking was inferior to that of the French—but it was different, as robust chianti is different from champagne.

La Varenne was forever cautioning his reader to "cook just long enough," while Scappi advocated medieval overcooking. Scappi presented the noble *maccaronis* (pastas) of Italian cooking in great variety; there were no *maccaronis* in *Le Vrai Cuisinier François*, though they were present in the earliest (fifteenth-century) English cookbooks.

The Italian influence was in fact felt more strongly in England, where macaroni (macrow to the English) and spicy forcemeats called "Balles of Italy" appear on fifteenth- and sixteenth-century English menus. But even the English rejected some of Scappi's dishes. Roast porcupine should have appealed to the rugged taste of the chief colonizers of America; indeed, it suggests the American frontier. But the sight of porcupine being sold in Italian markets shocked and repelled the Reverend John Ray, traveling through Italy in the 1660s. He refused to taste it, and was equally shocked by "Birds . . . in poulterer's shops . . . as in England no man touches, kites, buzzards, jayes, magpies and woodpeckers." La Varenne's many recipes for larks, pigeons, and ortolans demonstrate French preferences.

A statuette of a chef on the tomb of a 16th century Duke of Burgundy shows the flowing attire then worn by maistres-queux-porte-chappes *(robed master chefs).*

La Varenne's book was meant to guide young chefs to his own level of master chef, a goal hard to reach. The master chefs (*maître-queux*) were an elite corps permitted by Henry IV to form their own guild in 1599, *maître-queux-porte-chappes** (robed master chefs). The statue of a cook on the tomb of a sixteenth century duke of Burgundy shows the cook draped in a long robe; old drawings show that other kitchen hands wore tunics.

The master chefs would hire out only to the nobility and meant to keep their group undefiled by upstarts who might work for just anybody. A more basic reason for maintaining their exclusivity was, of course, the usual one—to keep themselves scarce in order to command higher wages.

An apprentice learned as much as he could through observation. With luck he might receive a helping hand from a more experienced apprentice, but rarely from a *maître-queux*.

---

*This ancient spelling of master or maître was dropped in the eighteenth century. The two spellings are used here interchangeably.

Traditionally that fellow's heart was as cold as aspic. He meted out information and encouragement about as readily as ortolans on toast.

"I know there are many who need the knowledge I am going to share," La Varenne wrote in his introduction. "Some of you have been denied information by expert cooks. Some of you may think you should know the answers and are shy to ask questions. Because I cherish my profession I feel it is my duty to share what little I know and spare aspiring cooks problems."

Noblesse oblige, perhaps? Little is known about La Varenne other than that he was chef to the Marquis d'Uxelles. He is thought to have died in Lyon around 1670. However, he is sometimes confused with Guillaume Fouquet, Marquis de la Varenne, who was born in 1560 and died in 1616. This earlier La Varenne won the confidence of Henry IV, served him on numerous diplomatic and romantic missions, and, according to the *Dictionnaire Historique de France,* was descended from a "family of serviteurs." Perhaps our La Varenne was descended from the same line. In any case, as long-time chef to the prominent Marquis d'Uxelles, our man was well qualified to instruct aspiring chefs in the ways of feeding the nobility, though what was fed them would be more analogous to home cooking today.

La Varenne made no claim to invention, but gathered together what by 1651 was common knowledge in noble French kitchens and bore the stamp of long practice.

A Cuisine Not Yet Haute

"A good meal ought to begin with hunger."

French proverb

T he reign of Louis XIV, longest reign of any French king, lasting from 1643 to 1715, conjures up visions of great luxury and glorious dining. This was true enough of the surroundings—stately halls hung with tapestries, tables draped in rich damasks and glittering with platters and goblets of gold and silver. But what was actually served at noble tables was uncomplicated food, simply prepared. The cuisine was wholesome rather than rich.

The elaborate sauces that fill pages in modern manuals for chefs did not yet exist. There were no basic sauces on which to build the varieties of sauces that could be counted in the hundreds a century and a half later.

La Varenne's sauces were usually based on the juices that flowed from the meat or fish during cooking. If it was deemed necessary to thicken this natural base, it was done with a liaison of eggs, ground almonds, or puréed mushrooms, or a combination of these, or by adding bread crumbs pushed through a sieve. However, the future *roux* could be discerned in the *liaison de farine* composed of butter, flour, onion, bouillon, and vinegar.

Only three sauces were described. *Poivrade* and *Robert* were tart combinations of onion, vinegar, spices, and pan juice. In somewhat altered form, both sauces are still included in the repertoire of French cuisine. *Robert* sauce, one of the most ancient sauces known, dates from at least the thirteenth century, when the Normans ruled England, and is mentioned in manuscripts of that time. The name is thought to be derived from "roebuck," a small deer.

A third sauce, the *sauce verte* (green sauce) that delighted Rabelais, appears in La Varenne's book but bears mention here only as a curiosity. There was nothing green about it except for the unripe wheat it included. Together with toasted bread crumbs, vinegar, salt, and pepper, the wheat was pounded in a mortar and then strained; this may have been used as a liaison.

A more useful liaison, which could perform today, was La Varenne's *jus de champignons.* "Take whole mushrooms with stems on. Be sure they are the youngest and the best. Put them in a pan with a little butter and bouillon; add an onion stuck with cloves, a scrap of roast meat, and a bouquet of herbs you may have handy. Season with salt and let the whole thing simmer gently until the mushroom juice is drawn. Then strain. You may add mushrooms and juice to all kinds of ragoûts and potages."

Mushrooms were used in many ways: as a dish by themselves—a ragoût, stuffed, or sautéed—or in conjunction with other dishes. The combination of pressed mushrooms and onions known as *duxelles* in classic French cuisine was apparently originated by La Varenne. He called it *champignons à l'olivier,* but it soon became known as d'Uxelles, probably after La Varenne's employer, the Marquis d'Uxelles. Eventually the apostrophe disappeared, but the preparation lives on in manuals for professional chefs and is still described almost exactly as La Varenne presented it.

His book was clearly a manual for chefs and he used the

telegraphic style still employed in modern guides for professionals. All the ingredients for a dish were given, the method of cooking was specified, but exact quantities were frequently omitted, deemed not necessary for professional cooks. It is the same today in Saulnier, Hering, Larousse, and Escoffier.

"Pastry is treated slightly here," he pointed out. "If you don't find all the different ways of making pastries, don't be surprised. I have not tried to make this book complete, but only to speak of the most necessary pastries usually employed in *entremets*." Evidently he already had in mind his next book, *Le Pastissier François*, published in 1653. (The Elzevir press reprinted the *Pastissier* in 1655 and a hundred years later it was the most sought-after Elzevir book—still is—because so few copies remained extant.) Though some recipes in *Le Vrai Cuisinier François* called for *feuilletée* (puff paste), a recipe for it was not included. La Varenne assumed that his reader could manage anything so basic without being led by the hand.

Feuilletée made the pastry shells that served as containers for food and were popular in all seventeenth-century cuisines, from England to Iberia. The French called them *abaisses* and *tourtes* and presented meats and fish in them: an entire salmon, for example, poached halfway to completion, then placed in a pastry shell shaped like a fish, seasoned with salt, pepper, lemon juice, and a crumbled bay leaf, dotted with butter and moistened with a few tablespoons of vinegar—enough to provide steam to finish cooking the salmon. A pastry top was added, pierced to allow steam to escape, and the dish was baked until the pastry turned golden.

Feuilletée also enveloped a well-seasoned cut of beef, braised beforehand, sprinkled with capers, then wrapped in the pastry and baked—an ancestor of Beef Wellington. This dish went by the name of *Bœuf à la Marotte* and was included among the recipes suitable for the battlefield, about the only place where seventeenth-century French noblemen would eat beef.

Like all chefs serving noblemen, La Varenne accompanied the Marquis d'Uxelles to the battlefield, where he also de-

13

Frontispiece of the very rare Le Pastissier Francois.

vised *Bœuf à la Chalonnoise.* This proves to be a pleasant variation of a brisket pot roast, braised in equal parts of bouillon
and vinegar with a bit of sage. As a final touch it was garnished with capers and served with fried turnips.

The French disdain for beef was countered by the English
preference for it. What should have bloomed into a royal
match failed even to bud when the Prince of Wales visited
France and displayed his English appetite to the Grande
Mademoiselle, cousin of Louis XIV. She rejected all thought
of marrying the future Charles II of England because "he ate
no ortolans and threw himself upon a piece of beef and
shoulder of mutton as if there were absolutely nothing else
to eat."

The mortar and pestle ground continuously, producing delicate fare for the French table. Forcemeats (*gaudiveau* then,
godiveau today) filled the cavities of small birds or were made
into quenelles to garnish platters. *Paste de gaudiveau* were
flaky, open pastry shells filled with lightly seasoned forcemeat
of capon livers, mushrooms and sweetbreads. Forcemeats of

fish were used in the same way, as a stuffing for whole fish or a filling for a tart. But, strangely, there is not a hint of *Quenelles de brochet* from La Varenne, though he supplied many recipes for cooking *brochet* (pike) in simpler ways: poached, roasted, baked, or *en ragoût*.

Even cod, *Morue à la Terre Nueve* (cod of Newfoundland), was not yet pounded into the notable *Brandade*, though the cod was already well established in French cuisine because Frenchmen had fished the waters off Newfoundland almost from the time of Cabot's discovery in 1497. La Varenne gave only the traditional recipe for *Morue salée* (salted cod), still one of the best ways to prepare it: poached, drained well, then sauced liberally with melted butter and garnished with chopped parsley.

Organs and variety meats were relished at the haughtiest French tables, as they still are, but *Menu doit de cerf* (minced reindeer toes) understandably failed to find a place in modern cookery. But at a time when hunting, along with warmaking, was of absorbing interest to noblemen, reindeer toes were considered a great delicacy, a "sporting dish," and were served as an *entremet.* side dish

Entremets had only recently found their way onto the French table. In earlier times *entremets* had been entertainments performed between courses by minstrels, jugglers, and actors, to interrupt the lengthy meals and allow diners to recharge their appetites. In the seventeenth century *entremets* became side dishes, distributed between the large platters of roasts, poultry, and fish. In either case the literal translation "between the dishes" applied. Today *entremets* are desserts.

Gelées, egg or cheese dishes, and various vegetables were also served as *entremets*, but vegetables were usually given some special treatment to qualify as *entremets*. Asparagus, already a favorite French vegetable, became an *entremet* by donning a simple sauce: the mashed cooked yolk of an egg mingled with vinegar and a dash of salt and nutmeg. *Asperges à la crème* was cold cooked asparagus cut into bite-size pieces and sauced with thick *crème* (commercial sour cream will do) combined with a raw egg yolk. This is a good way to use asparagus stalks of uneven length and scraggly appearance. Small cooked lima beans also make an agreeable cold side dish served in the same easy sauce.

Beets became an *entremet* sautéed with minced onion, then lightly baptized with vinegar. Cucumbers were prepared in the same way as the beets, then treated to a dash of nutmeg or finished with a hot vinegar and mustard dressing. Whole cucumbers were stuffed with a mixture of sorrel, eggs, and herbs and then braised. (Chopped spinach can substitute for the sorrel.) Small heads of garden lettuce, chicory, or celery became *entremets* when braised in bouillon. They are still prepared this way in classic French cuisine.

Most vegetables eaten today—with the exception of tomatoes and potatoes, which did not win acceptance in France until the late eighteenth century—were established in French cuisine by 1651. But the absence of any type of bean in La Varenne's book is puzzling. Some types of beans were known to most of Europe in ancient times, though the delicious *haricot vert* was not among them. This member of the bean family, the string bean, was native to North America and was transplanted to Europe by early explorers. It may have been growing in France by 1651 but perhaps was not yet popular.

By the eighteenth century the *haricot vert* was thoroughly naturalized. The French, constantly seeking the most tempting ways to prepare food, soon learned that the string bean was most succulent before it matured, and they picked it that way. Gardeners elsewhere can bring a reasonable duplicate of the French *haricot vert* to their table by picking string beans before they have matured fully.

The vegetable that caused a sensation in France was the pea. Introduced there early in the seventeenth century by France's ambassador to Holland, it was hailed as a kind of sweetmeat. Even Louis XIII shared in the excitement and personally tended and picked the vegetable in his gardens. At first eaten like bonbons, peas were soon devoured as if to satisfy a lustful craving, which may have been at the root of the spreading mania that continued into the eighteenth century. Peas had been praised as a sexual stimulant in *The Per-*

fumed Garden, a sixteenth-century manual of Arabian erotic techniques by Sheikh Al-Iman abd-Allah al-Nefzawi. The aphrodisiac recipe called for peas boiled with onions, then sprinkled with a mixture of powdered cinnamon, ginger, and cardamons.

Peas brought exorbitant prices because of their alleged properties and prompted one seventeenth-century writer to cry, "It is frightful to see persons sensual enough to purchase green peas at the price of fifty crowns per litron." As late as 1696 thrifty, sensible Madame de Maintenon wrote disapprovingly, "The pea business still goes on. Impatience to eat them, the pleasure of having eaten them, and the hope to eat more of them are the three questions constantly discussed by our princes. Several ladies, having supped—and supped well—went home and found more peas there to eat before going to bed, and ate them at the risk of indigestion. It is a fashion and the rage."

La Varenne was indifferent to the excitement and ignored the vegetable's alleged erotic properties. For him it was an excellent accompaniment to small birds, and when puréed made an attractive garnish for a platter.

At this time the influence of other countries on the French table was negligible. *Paste à l'Angloise* and *Œufs à la Portugaise* are the only foreigners in La Varenne's book. *Paste à l'Angloise* was a rabbit pie made with puff paste for which La Varenne specified "the freshest butter," pointing up the difference between French and Italian pastry making. The Italians made their puff paste with oil. *Œufs à la Portugaise* was actually Zabaglione, and may have originated in Iberia at that.

Except for *Crème à la Mazarin* and, possibly, *Bœuf à la Chalonnoise,* no dishes were connected to persons. That custom began later. The *crème,* actually the custard of *Œufs à la neige* without the meringue "eggs," may have been a nod to the Cardinal, or a dish that he favored. *Bœuf à la Chalonnoise* may have derived from the full name of La Varenne's employer, Louis Chalon de Blé, Marquis d'Uxelles.

After d'Uxelles was killed in battle in 1658, La Varenne continued to serve the widowed marquise, who became a prominent hostess and member of the spirited circle that formed around Louis XIV as a young king. Her name occurs frequently, along with those of Condé and Madames de Rochefoucauld and Coulanges, in the correspondence of Madame de Sévigné, who wrote of a d'Uxelles entertainment, "Nothing could surpass it for elegance. The company . . . the repast . . . everything deserved the highest praise."

Neither the marquis nor his distinguished chef is commemorated in any dish today. With the apostrophe gone from d'Uxelles the marquis sank into limbo. La Varenne fared no better, but the recent movement among some modern French chefs to "simplify" French cuisine is perhaps his epiphany.

Dining Under the Sun King

"'Tis an excellent thing to be a prince; he is served with such admirable variety of fare."

John Fletcher

When Louis XIV removed the court from the Louvre in Paris to the royal château at Versailles that his father had begun, he spent bankrupting funds to complete it and walled it in with protocol and etiquette beyond anything previously known. Gastronomically, the palace became a world unto itself, dominated by the tastes and desires of the monarch.

Louis XIV's move, made in 1682, might have augured ill for French cuisine. Louis's taste ran to limp, overcooked foods. Fortunately, among the higher nobility there were those who felt no compulsion to live in the king's shadow, and remained most of the time on their own estates where they dictated their own kitchen practices. Thus standards for taste and quality, traditionally emanating from the center of rule, flowed instead from two fountainheads. And a good thing it was for the future of gastronomy.

At Versailles Louis set new records for food consumption

with his prodigious appetite. All who observed him dining were filled with wonder. His sister-in-law, the Princess Palatine, wife of his brother the Duc d'Orléans often described his feats in her letters home, and in one she totted up the dishes she saw him consume at a single sitting: "four plates of different soups, a whole pheasant, a whole partridge, a large plate of salad, two big slices of ham, a dish of mutton in garlic sauce, a plateful of pastries, fruit, and hard-boiled eggs." No wonder his autopsy disclosed a stomach twice the normal size.

The princess had little right to criticize, according to other observers. She was a trencherman herself and her appetite was seldom appeased. Her yearning for the sauerkraut and smoked sausage of her homeland was often expressed in her letters, and by her standards the food from the Versailles kitchens was dainty.

When the court first moved to Versailles the kitchens were housed in a wing of the palace, divided into departments or "offices": bakery, stores and larder, beverages, cooking fuel, and a special office for the royal kitchen. Each office had its "officer of the mouth," to see that all ran smoothly.

When they were not preparing or serving meals, the kitchen help escaped from the hot kitchens into the palace courtyard, where their noisy conduct and rough language became a nuisance. This led to building the Grand Commun, away from the palace. The complex of four buildings, designed by Mansart, formed a handsome grouping around a courtyard, and had its own chapel where the kitchen staff could attend services. The chapel was dedicated to the thirteenth-century Franciscan monk St. Roch, who had devoted himself to tending the plague-ridden. He discharged his saintly protection well at Versailles, and became the patron saint of all cooks.

The move to the Grand Commun did little to relieve the slum-tenement atmosphere that hung over Versailles, despite its elegant architecture and gardens, its costly furnishings and its rigid etiquette. The courtyard still stank of the privies it played host to and the odor of manure still drifted over from the adjacent stables. But the kitchen noises were now muted.

At times two thousand servants were required to staff this vast cook house, which might be compared to the central headquarters of a fast-food emporium, able to disgorge tons of food at a set time. The kitchen staff got under way at daybreak to meet the sodden standards Louis XIV imposed on meats: he preferred boiled meats to roasted, except for ham, which he liked with a crisp, crackling skin stuck with cloves and sprinkled with cinnamon. He also liked crisp salad dressed with oil and lemon juice, and kept La Quintine, the royal gardener, busy producing greens. The gardener was renowned enough to be mentioned by contemporary writers, but no *chef de cuisine* in the royal kitchens seems to have earned this distinction, and in any case a gifted chef would have been wasted at Versailles, where everything, including dining, was second to etiquette.

Etiquette dominated the lives of all who lived at the palace. The entire day was structured to meet its requirements and consequently meal hours were strictly regulated. This was hard on the courtiers who swarmed through the palace, attending every public appearance of the king, seeking favors from those with influence, and busily turning every minute of the day to some personal profit. Often they were obliged to miss meals and forage around later for something to eat.

Dinner was the midday meal and Louis preferred to take this alone in his quarters. The evening meal, supper, was taken with the immediate royal family—the queen, the royal children and grandchildren—and was Louis's favorite meal. Though served inside the palace in the *grande appartement* and adjoining the king's private quarters, it was a "public" meal in that courtiers and visitors were free to observe the king and his family dining.

The same quarters were the scene of a grand reception three times a week, called an *appartement*. The Princess Palatine described one in a letter to the Electress of Palatine, dwelling, as was her custom, on the refreshments: "Four long tables laden with good cheer. All sorts of good things provided, including fruit tarts and sweetmeats. It looks just like the tables we set for Christmas eve. Beyond this is another room with four more tables . . . holding glasses and carafes with every sort of wine . . . after the eating and drinking . . . the company settle down, each to his favorite game, and you cannot imagine what a choice there is . . . this goes on until ten o'clock, when everyone goes to supper . . . It is certainly well worth seeing."

The Countess of Osnabruck, a visitor in 1679, found "these pleasures mixed with considerable discomfort . . . terribly crowded and hot." To Louis XIV they were an important ritual, as he immediately made clear to his daughter-in-law, the Dauphine, upon her marriage to the heir apparent. "Madame," he said, "you are to hold an *appartement* and to dance at it. We are not private people; we belong to the public."

Except for the *appartements,* where some informality was permitted, every act connected with eating in the presence of royalty was hedged in by rigid etiquette—even when royalty was not present. The king's meal received a doffed hat and a sweeping bow from any courtier who chanced to pass it on its way to the royal quarters.

At the dining table each move of a dish in the direction of royalty was governed by some rule, and the honor of tendering the dish or object was reserved for men of noble birth. The king's napkin reposed on a cushion like a holy relic. The cushion, in turn, was placed in an elaborate silver piece, a *nef,* fashioned in the form of a galleon complete with sails, and presented by the appointed noble when the king signaled. The same homage and service was rendered to the queen and to the princes and princesses royal. Publicly or privately, royalty did not open a napkin or pick up a glass unaided. In the absence of the ranking profferer, royalty would endure thirst rather than violate the rules of precedence.

Precedence was most important when it came to seating, if one was entitled to a seat, that is. At official functions a duchess could not sit in the same kind of chair that welcomed a princess's bottom. There were armchairs, armless chairs, and finally stools. "The divine tabouret," as Madame de Sévigné called it, was the first rung on the ladder of seating privilege. At such functions the right to occupy a seat of any kind belonged only to royal blood. Ordinary nobility stood, at meals as well as elsewhere, and aching feet were an occupational hazard of life at Versailles.

Along with excessive protocol and etiquette, Louis insisted on exquisite manners, which he himself practiced even to greeting the lowest chambermaid if he passed one in the corridor. It is therefore surprising that he ate with his fingers or a knife, spurning the recently introduced fork which was already in use at aristocratic Italian tables. Forks were in limited use in France as well, but so rarely employed that diners who fancied them carried their own. Louis owned a fork, engraved with his emblem of the rising sun, but refused to use it, probably for the same reason the English rejected it—too dainty for a man.

Obviously the court followed the king's lead, else why would Saint-Simon, that gossipy chronicler of court life under Louis XIV, comment on Louis's elegant use of the knife? "He used his knife with great skill, eating a chicken fricassee without staining anything but his fingers."

When the Duc de Burgoyne dared to use his fork at the royal table Louis rebuked him soundly. The Princess Palatine passed along this information in a letter, adding, "He would never have had the occasion to reproach me in that matter, for I have never in my life used anything to eat with but my knife and my fingers." This was true of people in high condition in most countries until well into the eighteenth century.

Louis ruled his table as absolutely as his kingdom but exerted little influence on the table away from Versailles. Those who hoped to rise in position and power fought to be domiciled in or near the palace—even a garret room under the royal roof was a prize to those who sought it—but many members of the ancient nobility preferred to live in Paris or in their nearby châteaux, appearing at court when the occasion demanded it.

Away from Versailles and its strangling etiquette the nobility led the relaxed life denied them at the palace, and certainly ate better. The letters and memoirs of seventeenth-century writers reveal a constant succession of social entertainments that outstrip the gaddings and most extravagant efforts of later monied society.

Madame de Sévigné, who embalmed much of the period in a correspondence of many years with her daughter, gave the palm for most magnificient host to the Prince de Condé, first cousin to Louis XIV. Condé's purse could bear the strain easily, but some nobles of less means who chose to compete with such magnificence, especially when they entertained the king, nearly pauperized themselves in the effort. Nicholas Fouquet, guardian of France's treasury in the early days of Louis's reign, nearly lost his life in the attempt.

The lavish fête that Fouquet staged at his magnificient estate, Vaux-le-Vicomte, was meant to dazzle the young king with his treasurer's hospitality. It came off so splendidly that it served instead to sharpen the royal eyes into relentless focus on the cost of such magnificence, and its possible source. Off to a dungeon went Fouquet, escorted by that legendary leader of the king's musketeers, D'Artagnan.

Soon afterward Madame de Sévigné described an even more extravagant entertainment given by—oh, the irony of it!—the Marquis de Seignelay, son of Fouquet's successor Jean-Baptiste Colbert. Colbert had helped to bring about Fouquet's downfall. The affair was made memorable for her by the eight thousand lanterns lighting the road from Versailles to the Seignelay fête, and indeed it was a gesture that had cost a small fortune. The *porte flambeaux* and *porte lanternes* had to be carried by licensed bearers who were usually hired to protect people going about after dark on foot or in sedan chairs. Their services came high.

The lighted road was described vividly, but Madame de Sévigné offered no details about the food served. Other sources reported that the dinner had required thirty-six cooks and assistants who used eighty saucepans, twenty huge boilers, and thirty spits.

Perhaps Madame de Sévigné's finicky appetite was put off by the laden tables that greeted her everywhere. By her own admission she was an abstemious eater who settled for "bread and butter seasoned with violets and herbs" on fast days, and relished a supper of "soup with a little butter . . . good prunes and good spinach." But she enjoyed the social activities and reported them faithfully. Her letters are a mirror of life among the nobility when they were free of the constraints of Versailles.

Social life was particularly active around her country estate near Paris, where partying proceeded at a fast clip and not all the laurels went to hosts. There were hostesses as well. Madame de Sévigné's close friend Madame de Chaulnes entertained often and one night diverted her guests with "an elegant supper with the comedy of Tartuffe after it . . . and then we had a ball [with] minuets and jigs." Another time at Madame de Chaulnes', "Two long tables [were] elegantly covered with sixteen dishes each, to which everyone sat down; and in this way they pass every evening. After supper some sat down to play, others chatted."

Sixteen choices for supper was a modest spread for those times; no wonder it pleased Madame de Sévigné. The lavish productions that usually comprised supper displeased her, and she thought that some of her friends served suppers too soon after dinner, which fashion now dictated should be served around two o'clock instead of at noon. To her daughter she wrote, "If foolish people would have me sup . . . at six, before my dinner is digested, I laugh at their proposals and let it alone until eight. And on what do you think I sup? Why, on quail or at most the wing of a partridge."

Partridges and all small birds, and fruit, were delectable fare to her. Whenever they graced a table she made a full report. One such entertainment was "the fullest and most elegant I have witnessed in a long time. The greatest rarities and choicest fruits in profusion: wood pigeons, quail, partridges, peaches, and pears as at Rambouillet." (The elegant table of the Marquise de Rambouillet shared renown with the brilliant conversation she sponsored at her *salons*.) Madame de Sévigné concluded "nothing is wanted but money to do everything."

Madame de Sévigné handled money carefully and had little

patience with friends who did not. She criticized the Princess de Tarente for "expensive entertainments that make me shudder at the consequences. I asked her what she meant by ruining herself and all her neighbors in fricassees and ragouts."

However, in most homes of her class the cost of entertaining was inconsequential. All employed large staffs known collectively as "officers of the mouth" and headed by a *maître d'hôtel* whose duties were spelled out in a manual: *Maître d'Hostel.*

"One takes for granted that homes that qualify for a *maître d'hostel* are grand homes," wrote the author, expending pages on how to keep an eye on the silver, linens, and utensils, the daily visit to the kitchen to see what food was on hand and what was to be purchased and the *maître d'*s responsibility to discharge that important task himself, thereby making certain that economy was exercised and seasonal delights obtained.

Dining procedures were carefully detailed: the placement of dishes, the order of service, and the highly visible assertion by the *maître d'* of his superiority. For starters he was told to "take a white napkin which he folds the long way and adjusts over his shoulder. This is the mark of his power and the particular symbol of his office. Now, to make it clear that his responsibility is considerable and that he does not give way, even to the *noblesse,* and to emphasize the true honor of his service, he wears a sword at his side, a cape hangs from his shoulders, a hat is on his head, but always the folded napkin is adjusted in the manner I have said."

Madame de Sévingné did not employ a *maître d'*. Her three homes were run on modest lines with limited staff and probably a *cuisinière* in the kitchen, though one is never mentioned in the correspondence, while other servants are. But she was on intimate terms with the most legendary *maître d'* of all—François Vatel (or Wattel), in the service of the Prince de Condé.

Before coming to Condé, Vatel had been *maître d'* to Nicholas Fouquet and had planned and executed the ill-advised fête that resulted in the treasurer's downfall.

Fouquet's bad luck had not bothered Vatel. From his point of view the affair had been a huge success. Was he to blame that in outdoing himself he had done in the treasurer? But when sufficient fish failed to arrive for a dinner that Condé, his new employer, was giving for the king and the royal entourage, *that* reflected adversely on *him*, Vatel—but let Madame de Sevigne tell the story:

"I am not yet recovered and hardly know what to write. Vatel, the great Vatel, late *maîstre d'hôtel* to M. Fouquet, and in that capacity with the Prince [Condé], a man so eminently distinguished for taste, and whose abilities were equal to the government of a State—this man, whom I knew so well, finding at eight o'clock this morning that the fish he had sent for did not come at the time he expected, and unable to bear the disgrace that he thought would inevitably attach to him, ran himself through with his own sword. Guess what confusion so shocking an accident must have occasioned. Think, too, that perhaps the fish might come in just as he was expiring. I make no doubt, the consternation was general."

A few days later she had more details. The three-day royal visit had apparently started out with a shortage of roast meat for the twenty-five tables the king's party required. Vatel, suffering from worry, strain, and sleepless nights, cried, "I have lost my fame! I cannot bear this disgrace!" Condé's assurance that meat had been plentiful at the king's table and the entire meal magnificent left him unmoved.

Madame de Sévigné describes Vatel, still sleepless, prowling the kitchen before dawn. Two loads of fish arrived—about half as much as had been ordered. Vatel cried out, "What! Is this all?" Told that it was he retired to his room and killed himself. Soon afterward more fish arrived.

There is another account of Vatel's suicide, by a courtier who was there, and it provides the vital fact that explains the neurotic Vatel's despair: it was Friday, a *jour maigre*: most guests would not eat meat that day.

Jean de Gourville, the courtier, was an aide to the Prince de Condé at the time and made himself out in his memoirs to be the hero of the day. He described how he hastily disposed of

Madame de Sevigne.

Vatel's corpse before the guests were up and stirring. The remains were bundled into a cart like so much garbage and driven off for hasty burial. Not a word was said to any of the guests and the consternation imagined by Madame de Sévigné did not occur. In de Gourville's account, he and

Condé had matters so well in hand "that no one had the slightest suspicion Vatel was not managing everything."

Vatel's immortality rests solely on his suicide: even his skill at planning brilliant fêtes is forgotten, though this earned him the fame he enjoyed during his brief lifetime of thirty-six years. He was not a chef, exerted no influence on cuisine, and has become a heroic figure because he could not face failure.

Louis Béchamel (or Béchameil) was anything but a heroic figure—on the contrary he was the occasional target of unkind jokes—but his contributions to gastronomy endure to this day. His title of *maître d'* to Louis XIV's brother, the Duc d'Orléans, was honorary. As in all royal households, the privilege of service was conferred in name only; the actual duties were discharged by a professional. One may be sure that Béchamel, deviser of the sauce that bears his name and of the classic *vol-au-vent*, took his honorary title seriously and interested himself in the activities of the *maître d'* and the *chef de cuisine*.

His flair for the exquisite and tasteful had brought him to the attention of Louis XIV soon after he gained entry to court circles through his fortunate marriage to the daughter of Colbert, the king's treasurer. Louis entrusted him with the beautification of the palaces at St. Cloud and Marly.

Unfortunately, Béchamel's artistic talent was often outweighed by his fatuity and vanity. Some nobles found him irritating, others poked fun at him. The prankish Comte de Gramont was more annoyed than most because he had learned that Béchamel thought there was a resemblance between them. Gramont did not agree.

Walking in the Tuilleries one day, Gramont saw Béchamel strolling ahead. He nudged his companion and whispered, "I'll wager you that I can boot that fool on his backside and he'll take it as a compliment." When the blow landed Béchamel turned, shocked. "Oh, excuse me," said Garmont. "I thought you were my nephew—my exact likeness, you know." Béchamel smiled happily, took Gramont's arm, and walked off with him. The incident found its way into the memoirs of Saint-Simon, whose exhaustive chronicle of life at Versailles shows how boring the routine of court life was, as compared to the vivacity away from it that Madame de Sévigné reported.

When, toward the end of his reign, Louis came under the influence of the assertively virtuous Madame de Maintenon, the court pace changed. The glamor that had made it a model for other courts to copy diminished greatly. Overfed and overbled as he was, Louis set a slower tempo. He absented himself from the *appartements,* now less well attended, though the same overwhelming platters proceeded to the royal quarters. His intimate courtiers no longer vied to entertain him at their estates, though they continued to entertain each other lavishly.

In the thirty years that Madame de Maintenon was his wife, Louis relaxed into a domesticity more suitable to a comfortable burgher than a Bourbon king, sitting at a cozy fireside, chatting with a woman who had never wished to play the coquette. Perhaps it was her comfortable presence that gave Madame de Maintenon her power over the king. Perhaps it was her reassurance to the unflagging male in him.

Louis was a robust man in every way, and it is said that he exercised his connubial rights daily almost to the time of his death. Madame de Maintenon, to judge by the woman revealed in her correspondence and the fact that she was three years older than Louis, an aging woman as Louis was an aging man, would seem more likely to have banked such fires rather than fanned them. In her early fifties she had complained to her confessor that "it would be hard to imagine to what degree husbands extend their demands."

There is no doubt about Louis's appetite for food. It never slackened until the last days of his life, though he welcomed occasional spurring. In the last few years of his life Madame de Maintenon devoted herself to accomplishing this and is supposed to have invented *cutlets Maintenon* to tempt him: a rack of lamb, well charred on the outside, with the outer chops discarded at the time of serving, leaving only the pink interior to be eaten.

Cutlets Maintenon lives on in modern *haute cuisine*, but in name only. The dish bears no resemblance to its original namesake. Now the rack is cooked on one side, then partly slit to admit a stuffing of mushrooms cooked in butter. Then, with the slit closed tightly, the rack is cooked on the other side.

When Louis XIV died in 1715, his great-grandson, next in the line of succession—death having removed all those closer to it—became Louis XV. He, like the two previous Louis, was five years old at the time of accession. It would be some time before he could make the court the lively place it had once been under Louis XIV. Meanwhile, and as always, the passage of time brought new blood to the social scene. Younger men now took the lead in pursuit of a life filled with pleasure. Foremost among them was the regent, Philippe Duc d'Orléans.

Saturnalias
Enlarge
the Cuisine

*"Cookery is become an art, a
noble science; cooks are
gentlemen."*
Robert Burton

T he impetus for enlarging French cuisine after its
initial introduction to the world in 1651 came
out of a dissolute court led by a libertine regent.

Philippe d'Orléans, nephew of Louis XIV, arrogated to
himself the total powers of the regency during Louis XV's
minority, despite Louis XIV's stipulation that a ten-member
regents' board was to govern. The result, as Louis had feared
and sought to avoid, was an era of abandonment and de-
pravity.

Like the earlier English Restoration, the eighteenth-century
Regency was a revolt against enforced decorum. But the Regency was also rejecting the hypocritical propriety which
Louis XIV had demanded even before he came under the
influence of prim Madame de Maintenon. Not that intrigues
and scandals had been banished from Louis XIV's court by
his insistence on discreet conduct. Under his stern disap-
proval such affairs could only be guessed at, while under the
easygoing regent they were openly exposed.

Etiquette and protocol sagged and the court had not been so lax since the days of Henry IV, the ancestor Philippe seemed determined to emulate. In her steady flow of letters to her native Palatine, the regent's mother ascribed it to the inertia of her son's wife and daughter, both of whom she despised. "The wife is so lazy she is never able to do the slightest thing; she lies on a sofa all day and [the daughter] does likewise at Luxembourg. So you see, there cannot be any court."

What shocked her was laughably innocent. "Hardly any women come to see me these days," she wrote, "because I cannot and will not allow them to appear before me without stays and wearing scarves and loose garments." She seemed unaware that much more was loose than garments, but other correspondents and memoirists gave more explicit details of the debauchery led by her son.

Philippe is an ambivalent figure, dealt with gently by some historians as a kindly, democratic leader who sought to diminish the autocratic rule Louis XIV had imposed, and to restore to the nobility some of its lost powers. Others see him as indolent and permissive.

Philippe's most ardent supporters do not deny that sensuality ruled him. His erotic urges were rumored to run the scale from homosexuality to incest, the latter with his daughter, the Duchess of Brunswick. Actually, he responded to everything that appealed to the senses—poetry, music, painting (he made Watteau court painter and ushered in the rococo style)—and more than to any of these he responded to food properly prepared. A dish seductive to the eye and palate could give him orgiastic gratification.

Court dining under him was far removed from the endless ceremonial dinners which had been the rule under Louis XIV, when the heavy, overcooked foods favored by the king were served in gluttonous quantities. Philippe returned to the lighter cuisine dictated by La Varenne and advanced it further by his own demands.

The succulent but crisp birds, the airy *frigandeaux* and *godiveaux* now reappeared, but most important were the new

An intimate souper in the 17th century. Engraving by Moreau le Jeune.

culinary inventions that foreshadowed the classic cuisine of the nineteenth century. Many additions to the culinary repertoire were concocted by Philippe's intimate circle, whose members were scornfully labeled *roués* (the females *rouées*) after *roué*, the torture wheel. Because of the popular suspicion that orgies were their chief pastime, many Frenchmen thought the wheel would be a fitting treatment for the entire pack. Orgies aside, there is no doubt that cookery was a favorite indulgence behind the guarded doors of the regent's private quarters.

The coterie would prepare the entire meal for themselves, with the affair taking on the spirit of a knightly tournament to win a monarch's favor. Pots and turnspits substituted for steeds, and ladles replaced lances. The regent was often both judge and participant, originating exotic combinations of carp roe with poultry or other fish, or giving a medieval twist to a haunch of venison by soaking it in wine and garnishing it with Seville oranges. Noteworthy among the inventions were *Pains à la d'Orléans*. These may have been molded forcemeats, but then again they may have been souffle-like preparations served in a *pain* or bread croustade. The delicacies were enjoyed at the *petit soupers* which the regent also introduced.

When Philippe removed the court from Versailles to Paris on the pretext that the climate of Paris was better for the young king, Parisians quickly took up the court's enthusiasm for cooking. To excel at it became the rage among the bourgeoisie as well as the nobility. Women past the age of coquetting found that they could still charm successfully with a superb ragout. Expert swordsmen could command as much respect for their seasoning as for their foils.

Entertaining again reached levels of extravagance that recalled the spectacular fêtes at Vaux and Chantilly in the early days of Louis XIV's reign. The Duchess of Brunswick, as expert as her father the Duc d'Orléans at such matters, ruled over a table famed for its lavish quantity as well as quality. One such dinner, served in February 1718, gives some idea of her bounty.

In the style of those times the meal was divided into "services" or "removes," with all dishes for the particular service placed on the table at one time. The first service led off with thirty-one potages, thirteen entrées of meat and fish (platters of large roasts and whole fish), and thirty-two hors-d'oeuvres (dishes similar to *entremets*).

This was only a preliminary sortie. In the second service the dishes came on like a battalion, to confront the serious eaters—one hundred and thirty-two hot dishes flanked by sixteen cold dishes and seventy-two *entremets*.

The concluding dessert service presented one hundred large platters of fresh fruits arranged in pyramids, ninety-five dishes of cooked fruits, fifty dishes of sugared delicacies, and a hundred and six compotes laden with marzipan dainties and other sweetmeats.

Staff to aid the guests was equally lavish. The duchess's army of retainers was said to number eight hundred and included a large corps of footmen, making it an easy matter to position one behind each diner's chair, ready to flit to a far corner of the table to obtain any dish the guest desired. Instant gratification was demanded by the debauched society of the Regency. The debauchery was contained, however, within the narrow perimeters of the court. The bourgeoisie, securely bound by their moderate standards, frowned upon the dissipation but looked with envy on its trappings, particularly the pleasure it brought to dining. What they envied was obtainable enough, if a title was obtained first.

Bourgeois Gentlemen Advance the Cuisine Further

"Man lives on good soup and not on fine words."

Molière

When Philippe d'Orléans died in 1723 and Louis XV became king in fact at age thirteen, and a husband two years later, he followed in the easygoing ways of the regent. This was encouraging to ambitious members of the bourgeoisie who longed to become part of the new nobility that had grown up lushly since the days of Louis XIV.

A title had become a kind of commodity exchanged for services to the king, a practice that had begun much earlier but that Louis XIV had greatly advanced. The procedure was usually in three stages: the purchase of an impressive estate; followed by the purchase of a public office (all were for sale and the office would automatically provide entry into fringe court circles); and finally the coveted prize. Louis XIV had dispensed titles freely when the services rendered warranted it, or if the seeker's wealth was sufficient, but he had tried to give at least the appearance of hard-won to the titles he granted by maintaining social barriers at court. These had eroded greatly during the nine years of the Regency and continued to weaken under Louis XV. At the doors to the throne room, however, they still held fast against all who could not prove noble descent back to 1400. This device helped somewhat to control the advancing tide of new titles, although the outer edges of the court now swarmed with the new nobility, later described by Madame de Staël as "those gentlemen of the second class whose patents are made out overnight." According to her backward glance at Louis XV's court, there were only "two hundred old historic families" who could prove their nobility dating back to 1400, "but a hundred thousand of the new nobility."

The original nobility separated themselves as much as possible from the newly ennobled, and these worthies, in turn, were insufferable to the bourgeoisie from whose ranks they had so recently graduated. The latter responded with resentment and a tightening of *their* pecking order. The Paris bourgeoisie scorned the provincial bourgeoisie—a popular play of the time had a Parisian lady exclaim, "What! does he take me for a provincial?"—and the bourgeoisie, who "lived nobly," that is who did not engage in a trade or profession, scorned them both. Throughout the entire structure "nothing was more marked than the hierarchy of bourgeois society," to quote a contemporary observer, Antoine-Augustin Cournot.

The striving and petty distinctions of this society had been a favorite target for Molière's satire in the seventeenth century. In *The Misanthrope* he took a swipe at the social assaults they made via the table.

CLITANDRE: But young Cleon, whom the most respectable people go to see. What say you of him?
CÉLIMÈNE: That it is to his cook he owes this distinction, and to his table that people pay visits.

Voltaire continued the process in the eighteenth century, sharpening his wit on the bourgeoisie. But at times, in a fit of reversal, he seemed to revel in the luxurious life they enjoyed, especially the petit bourgeoisie of Paris. "What makes Paris the most flourishing city in the world is not the

One of the most successful bourgeoisie: Samuel Bernard, who became Comte de Goubert. From a portrait by Hyacinthe Rigaud.

large number of its magnificent and opulent mansions replete with every luxury, but the vast number of private houses, in which people live in a state of comfort unknown to our ancestors, and at which other nations have not yet arrived . . . Our notary, lawyer, tailor, is far better lodged . . . and is far better waited on than any magistrate in the capital of England. More poultry and game is eaten in Paris in one day than in a week in London . . . in no other city in the world does a larger number of citizens enjoy so much abundance of all good things . . . and so pleasant an existence."

Some effort went into attaining this "pleasant existence," much of it directed to social conquests which, one hoped, would yield a profitable return in business channels. The same techniques that work in the social hierarchies of today's society worked as well then. Talent or marked ability were useful assets; money combined with these assets could work wonders, as Samuel Bernard, the celebrated financier under Louis XIV, had demonstrated.

Bernard's table had set new records for extravagance. "For dinner alone his table cost him 150,000 livres per year," the eighteenth-century historian Barbier reported. That was a princely level and warranted the title of Comte de Goubert, which the financier soon acquired. To add to his social success, he married his sons into the older "new" nobility and later, as a widower, crowned his achievements by marrying the daughter of the haughty Comte de Boulanvilliers, a title of the first rank. In a way it was a marriage of poetic justice. Boulanvilliers had openly scoffed at Bernard's climb to social success as a noted host, and had vowed that no member of the Bernard family would ever enter his. To other bourgeois, Bernard's success was compelling evidence of what money could buy, if a bourgeois knew how to spend it.

The Regency and the reign of Louis XV were prosperous times. Foreign trade and shipping increased; manufacturing grew; services of every kind were in greater demand. Whether bankers or tailors, members of the bourgeoisie who pursued social or business success took to the table to achieve their ambitions. The greater number of hosts and the accelerated competition to surpass at table widened the culinary boundaries.

In 1739 the publication of a three-volume work, *Les Dons de Comus* (Gifts of the God of Joy), revealed to what extent these boundaries had stretched and the enormous strides French cuisine had made since its first formal appearance in 1651. At that time La Varenne had produced his work for professional chefs. Marin, the author of *Les Dons de Comus*, did not ignore the *chef de cuisine*, but he wanted it known that *his* work was mainly for *"le public éclairé,"* the enlightened public.

The public was the bourgeoisie but Marin avoided the term. In 1746 another chef, Menon (the first names of both men are unknown), followed in Marin's tracks and enjoyed considerable success by titling his less pretentious book *La Cuisinière Bourgeoise*. In bourgeois kitchens a *cuisinière* was usually in command. Male *chefs de cuisine* continued to hold themselves above such employment. "Only houses of the first class kept men cooks, and more than half the magistrates were content with female cooks," says the historian Charles Ducros. The ascendancy in France of female cooks began at this time, and with *Les Dons de Comus* at hand, the mysteries of the *chefs de cuisine* were revealed to the less experienced.

Marin was *chef de cuisine*, and later *maître d'hôtel* as well, to the Prince de Soubise, Marechal of France. This is probably recommendation enough as to his qualifications. The Prince de Soubise was a gastronome of the first order, noted for his superb table at which he spared no expense to gratify his own or a guest's appetite for the exquisite—especially if the guest was the king himself. He is forever enshrined in gastronomy by an onion sauce bearing his name, though at its first appearance, in Marin's work, it was known as *sauce au Duc* (duc and marquis were also titles the name of Soubise held claim to). *Sauce au Duc* was one of seventy-nine sauces that *Les Dons de Comus* presented, evidence that the proliferation of sauces was one of the most conspicuous developments in French cuisine since La Varenne's meager few.

The roux base of 1651, *liaison de farine*, had become, with the addition of milk, *sauce Béchamel*. Béchamel sauce may have been going the rounds for nearly fifty years, but now it appeared with the name of its deviser, already known for his architectural contributions to the royal palaces. Other by now familiar names were to be found under sauces—*allemande, espagnole, suprême, hollandaise*—though none of these were made as they are today.

New methods and recipes were presented which Marin asserted had only recently been created. "Please observe," he said of *Pigeons à la lune.* "This method of preparing pigeons is scarcely known as yet." The birds were braised until almost tender, then removed from the cooking pan and placed on a heatproof earthenware platter where they would finish cooking. But first a farce made of whatever the chef had handy in the kitchen—poultry, veal, sausage, or a combination of them all—was spread over the entire surface of the bird except for the breast. For this Marin specified a farce of chicken livers, sweetbreads and truffles, to be covered with a thin pastry cut in the shape of a heart "or whatever you fancy." The birds were then returned to the oven briefly to finish cooking.

Many dishes required similar painstaking touches, often meant to disguise what really lay underneath. What appeared to be a bird might actually be a ham; what seemed to be solid meat collapsed under cutlery. Surprise was an ingredient of many dishes.

Ramequins soufflés, a soufflé baked in a pastry shell, may have been a version of the Regency *pains d'Orléans.* The soufflé mixture appears to be the ancestor of modern soufflés, though made by a different method. It began with an uncooked base composed of *pâté royal* (choux paste), combined with cheese, egg yolks, and herbs, thoroughly blended in a *mortier.* The beaten egg whites were then folded in, and the soufflé was distributed among the waiting pastry *ramequins.* Into a hot oven they went, where, said Marin, "You will soon see them mount before your eyes."

A number of recipes were labeled *à la Polonnoise*, because the Polish princess Marie Lescinska was now queen of France, but they bore no resemblance to present-day *polonaise,* which is a garnish of riced hard-boiled eggs and fried bread crumbs, usually topping asparagus or cauliflower. The eighteenth-century *Polonnoise* combined parsley, onions, shallots, butter, salt, pepper, and a dash of ginger with a cup of white wine and the juice of a lemon. It was not used on the two vegetables associated with it today, though, curiously, a sauce strongly resembling the modern *polonaise* appears as *sauce petites œufs perles:* crumbled egg yolks and finely minced shallots, combined with a little consommé and heated briefly. It was used on poultry and proves to be not a bad idea at that—and on broiled fish or veal as well.

Some culinary influence might have been expected of Marie, as the daughter of King Stanislaus of Poland. By hearsay Stanislaus was a leading gastronome who invented the *baba,* a sweet yeast cake, prepared at that time with saffron and soaked in wine. He may have borrowed a few notions from French cuisine. *Oeufs farcis frits* (stuffed cooked eggs, fried) is an interesting recipe in *Les Dons de Comus* that later embellished a Polish dish. And the *sauce petites oeufs perles* somehow became transformed into *à la Polonaise.*

No contributions from Marie are evident. Nor did she introduce lentils to France as historian Ducros states, adding that before then lentils were considered fit food only for horses. They were relished by Frenchmen, highly placed Frenchmen at that, long before Marie was born. La Varenne provided recipes for their use fricasseed, puréed and sautéed. Marin described a variety called *à la Reine* which he explained "came from the Auvergne and has an excellent flavor." His recipes were basically like those of La Varenne, but more detailed. *Lentilles fricassées* and *lentilles à l'huile* are interesting ways to present this ancient staple food.

Apparently Marie took little interest in culinary matters, though she had a hearty appetite, but Louis's interest increased. It may have been only coincidence, but his interest in Marie slackened as he developed into a bon vivant. He had been interested enough in the beginning. Marie was seven years older than Louis, and to a lad of fifteen she was ripe womanhood personified. The marriage was hailed as a great success, though before her arrival one contemporary writer mourned, "Now we will have a queen whose name ends in 'ski.'" The details of royal wedding nights were important information to the court and public, and the morning following the nuptial Marshal Villars let it be known that the king's prowess "was worthy of the finest stud cadet at St. Cyr."

Though she was a colorless queen, plain as oatmeal, Louis remained constant for seven years, clearly satisfied with her other attributes. After that his gaze wondered elsewhere as he became the leader of the inventive gourmands of his reign. Surrounded by these courtiers he entertained at intimate *petits soupers* where he and the guests prepared most of the food. Such exotic dishes as pigs' tongues stuffed with jelly and pheasant stuffed with carp forcemeat were born of these evenings.

She may have attended the *soupers* at the beginning, but Marie was soon absent from the merry gatherings as the king's affections shifted elsewhere. One by one, over a period of thirteen years, his mistresses were the titled Neslé sisters, a brood of five, three of whom were openly acknowledged as mistresses.

Then the epitome of bourgeois ambitions materialized. Louis XV came under the spell of pretty Madame d'Etoiles. A bourgeois could acquire a title, but could a bourgeoise acquire a crown? Anything seemed possible after Madame de Maintenon's marriage to Louis XIV. Bourgeois ambitions soared. Madame d'Etoiles progressed no further than official mistress to the king, but as Madame de Pompadour she wielded more power and influence than any bourgeoise had dreamed possible. Under her patronage all the arts flourished—cuisine among them. Soon all bore the unmistakable imprint of the rococo, its development now fostered by her.

The Rococo Table

"A very fantastical banquet
Just so many strange dishes."

Anonymous

Madame de Pompadour has been called the "queen of rococo," and in essence this was true. Though the rococo began to emerge during the Regency and was already established as a mode by the time she became the king's official mistress, she reigned over its most fertile period and brought it to harvest. The table received its full share of her attention.

She was the product of a comfortable bourgeois background and the wife of a rich young bourgeois gentleman, M. d'Etoiles, whose means and her social talents combined well. Pretty, graceful, with a pleasing voice and a modest talent for the clavichord, she moved easily in the society of wealth and power with its sprinkling of literati. With a handsome château for background she entertained important people and began the obligatory social climb of her class.

In the course of this ascent she came to Louis XV's attention. In 1745 she was installed at Versailles as his official mis-

Madame de Pompadour, by Boucher.

tress, to the annoyance of most ladies at court. A bourgeoise upstart, they sneered. In 1752 Louis gave her the title Duchess of Pompadour and an estate to match. It had not been easy.

Court society shut her out at first by striking at her ignorance of their shibboleths—the catchwords and verbal affectations employed by closed societies everywhere. The Duc de Luynes reported, "She was not familiar with the language used among people she was unaccustomed to." Voltaire had known her as wealthy Madame d'Etoiles and helped her over this hurdle; he coached her to sustain the diphthong in *roi* and *moi* and weeded out the bourgeois phrases that court society shunned like the pox.

There was little Madame de Pompadour could do to combat her rumored ancestry: a provisioner for a great-grandfather and a butcher for a grandfather. Nor could she alter her family name of Poisson, which provoked scornful jests and caricatures and the venomous *poisonnades*, insulting verses circulated by her enemies at court. Pompadour, if not indifferent to these slurs, was at least defiant. She collected replicas of fish in semiprecious materials, decorated precious trinkets and objets d'art with them, and emblazoned fish on the bindings in her fabulous library.

She surrounded herself with all the trappings of royalty. A chevalier of high birth rode as equerry alongside her carriage; noblemen carried her mantle and served her at table; and her chambermaid, Madame du Hausset, was a lady of quality who became a minor-league Saint-Simon, setting down chatty accounts of daily happenings at court. One account dealt with a chef discovered outside the king's apartments. The poor fellow, employed at a nearby château, was on his way to visit a fellow chef in the royal kitchens and had lost his way. Luckily another palace servant recognized him, vouched for him, and for his cooking as well, "He makes the best *bœuf à l'écarlate* in the world." This pickling process, employing saltpeter, turned the beef red and produced the corned beef known today. It also made the meat more acceptable on upper-class French tables at the time.

Most of Madame du Hausset's memoirs were concerned with Madame de Pompadour's private life, and they revealed her as an apprehensive woman, fighting every inch of the way to keep her royal lover content at her side. She dosed herself with what she hoped were aphrodisiacs—ambergris in her morning chocolate, truffles and celery soup for dinner—to combat her frigidity.

If the king appeared bored she invented antidotal entertainments. Frequently these were rustic fêtes at the royal châteaux, and at one she staged a group wedding for several couples from surrounding villages.

To contrast with these crowded affairs she entertained him with intimate dinners for two at her small private pavilion, the Hermitage, where they often prepared their own food as a lark. One dinner worthy of comment was prepared at Saint-Hubert by the king and the Ducs de Gontaut, de Coigny, de La Valliere, and de Fleuri. The king scored handsomely with his *Poulets au basilic* (herbed chicken), poultry roasted with a

Menu and estimated cost of the food for a dinner
or supper to be served to Louis XV and his Polish
queen.

mixture of herbs, predominantly basil, in the cavity. Chopped basil was applied to the outside of the bird (brushed with egg for adherence) before roasting was completed, and the dish was removed from the oven before the herbs lost their greenness. Parsley was already being used in this way, applied to a coating of egg and butter just before the roasting was completed. To substitute basil for parsley was the King's idea.

At these informal meals all leftovers were served to the attending pages by the titled chefs. With true *noblesse oblige* Louis XV prepared and served the coffee to his friends and attendants, a ritual he often performed, fancying himself an accomplished brewer of coffee and tea.

Madame de Pompadour encouraged his culinary creativity and sought new delights for his table as zealously as she encouraged the development of the arts and crafts, and for the same reason—to please and entertain him. She established the porcelain factories at Sèvres, encouraged cabinet makers into curving the lines of furniture and sponsored the painters who came to exemplify the era—Boucher, Fragonard, Nattier, de la Tour.

She constantly hounded her excellent chef, M. Benoit, to invent new excitements for the table as well. *Filets de volaille à la Pompadour*—boned chicken breasts, flattened and rolled around a forcemeat of sweetbreads, then tied securely and braised in a rich bouillon—is often mentioned in connection with her. As a recipe it was like dozens of others in vogue at that time, and was probably judged to be memorable because of the chef's skill in preparing it.

The pressure on chefs to be inventive was great, but at the palace, if the contents of tureens and platters sometimes lacked novelty, *tables volantes* could rise, literally, to the rescue in a burst of rococo fantasy, hoisted from the floor below and completely set for dining.

The royal emphasis on dining inspired Menon to produce a culinary work which he called *Les Soupers de la Cour* (1755), stocked with much the same recipes Marin had introduced, with here and there a simple variation—eggs stuffed with cucumber purée, for example. Sixteen years earlier, when Marin revealed the great progress made by French cuisine since La Varenne first put it on record, he had not claimed that it was new or different, only that it was broader. But gradually it had come to be called new, modern, changed, and in general a great step forward. A scholarly article by M. G. Osterman, *La Cuisine Changée, Culina Mutata*, called it a milestone in France's cultural development.

In a later review of its progress, Louis Sébastien Mercier wrote, "Dishes today are lighter and have greater subtlety. We have learned the secret of eating more and better, and digesting it more rapidly. The new cuisine is good for our health and will prolong our lives."

Though its preparation was delicate, the "new cuisine" was

often rich and bedizened. Even its preparation was conducted in cooking pots fine enough to ornament the table itself. Silver cooking utensils were used in the royal kitchens, and in others that were merely bourgeois, as a recipe for *Poulets en papillote* indicates. Pieces of chicken were covered with a farce of mushrooms and livers, chilled, then wrapped in paper and roasted. "However, if you don't wish to wrap them in paper," read the recipe, "prepare them the same way and roast them in a silver dish, lightly covered."

Beyond doubt the kitchen that cooked in silver served a dining table that glittered with more of it. In Mercier's opinion this was a logical corollary to the cuisine's advancement. "The *luxe* of a table service is an infallible indication of the progress of cuisine," he declared.

Arthur Young, an English agriculturist who traveled through France later in the century, was impressed by the table service of his hosts and found silver even on the tables of Bordeaux hotels. He had only praise for the cuisine itself and declared the French table superior to any to be found in England, praise difficult to pry from an Englishman in the eighteenth century.

But the cuisine had its detractors among Frenchmen. Especially among those who experienced it in its highest form. The Comte d'Argenson blamed it for the frequent bouts with indigestion which now plagued Louis XV. Voltaire disliked the culinary fantasies, the disguises that foods now wore. In a letter to the Comte d'Autrey he complained, "I swear my stomach cannot accept this 'new cuisine.' When I entertain you it will be with a nice old-fashioned meal containing no surprises. I cannot tolerate sweetbreads swimming in a sea of sauce; I detest biting into what appears to be a portion of meat and finding it to be two kinds of rabbit and mostly turkey. I like food plain. The old sages said it is best for you. And I like a crust on my bread!" Evidently the crusty French bread so beloved today did not exist yet, or had it been exiled in the interest of daintiness?

Voltaire preferred plain food, but this was not true for all men of letters. Many gathered regularly around tempting feasts, prepared to relish both the dishes set before them and

Frontispiece for a volume of etchings created for Madame de Pompadour by Boucher. Frontispiece also by Boucher.

the words that filled the air. Daily, the *philosophes* spent a good part of their waking hours at the table in an eighteenth-century version of the ancient *Deipnosophists* (Banquet of the Learned) and prepared for these encounters with great care.

Jean-Francois Marmontel describes a meal at the table of Madame de Tencin as a draining experience, more exhausting than a physical contest, and like one in many ways. "I could see that all the wits and intellectuals gathered there had arrived to engage in a competition for which they had carefully prepared, and their need to vie sometimes diverted the natural course of conversation. They would quickly seize the right moment—like seizing a ball in the volley of conversation—to place their anecdote or maxim, or make their point. Sometimes it fell outside the boundaries. Marivaux was such a contender, always impatient to demonstrate his finesse and sagacity. Montesquieu invariably waited for the ball to come to him."

The Abbé Bernardin de Saint-Pierre compared these

encounters to combats between gladiators. And what a collection of intellectual participants they were: Buffon, Rousseau, Voltaire, Diderot, and Raynal. Raynal, a leader among French free-thinkers, used these dinner gatherings to air his views against the exploitation of the West Indies natives. His views did not impair his appetite for turtle soup, a West Indian newcomer to French tables.

Madame de Pompadour was on friendly terms with many of these intellectuals. They, in turn, admired her wit, superb taste, and support of the arts, particularly her interest in the work of the encyclopedists led by Diderot. The Comte de Buffon, director of the royal gardens and the royal museum, visited her frequently at Versailles and paid his compliments. Voltaire was her devoted friend until a rift occurred between them, which Madame du Hausset described in her memoirs.

The irreverent, witty *philosophe* was present when Madame de Pompadour was served a quail that she complained was too plump, *grassouillette*. Voltaire approached her and said, loud enough for others present to hear, "*Grassouillette, entre nous, me semble un peu caillette. Je vous le dis tout bas, belle Pompadour*" (*Grassouillette*, between ourselves, seems to me a little *caillette*. Let me tell you quietly, lovely Pompadour.)

Very likely Voltaire was exercising his wit with a pun, saying that *grassouillette* was the language of a *caillette* a Paris gossip. *Caillette* is also the diminutive for quail. Pompadour, who probably knew that her enemies at court sometimes referred to her as the *caillette de Paris* (could Voltaire not have known?), rightfully took it as an impertinence. Madame du Hausset recalled that Madame de Pompadour was chilly to Voltaire from that day on.

Madame de Pompadour's ties to the literary fraternity, and her interest in the arts, continued to absorb her when her role as official mistress no longer required her to perform its primary function. She was glad to relinquish that responsibility; she made no secret to her close friends of her frigidity. Nevertheless she continued to concern herself with the king's comfort in that respect, especially as she did not want to be supplanted by another official mistress. Always alert to his needs, she continued to keep a watchful eye on his table and entertainment, but now she also supplied him with new morsels for his bed, helping to stock his private hideaway, *le Parc au cerfs*, with a constantly changing supply of comely young women, kept on hand like so much fresh fruit, to slake the royal appetite.

She performed her duties well. When she died, in 1764, Louis XV mourned her deeply. For three years he contented himself with *le Parc au cerfs*, but after that he settled back into a more regular routine with his second bourgeois mistress, the daughter of a cook.

Madame du Barry, from a painting by Drouais. Could the coffee in her cup have been brewed by Louis XV?

The Daughter
of a Cuisinière

*"A man is in general better
pleased when he has a good
dinner upon his table, than
when his wife talks Greek."*

Samuel Johnson

I t was easy for Jeanne Bécu Beauvarnier du Barry
to maintain the standard that Madame Pompadour had established for Louis XV's table. She could plan a
meal of royal plenitude, and if need be she could prepare it
herself. She had the flair that blesses the natural-born cook,
and what was not instinctive she had learned from her
mother, cook to a prosperous bourgeois family.

Her chief talent, however, was demonstrated in the
boudoir. There, it is said, she outstripped all her predecessors
because of her superb and extensive training as a kind of
eighteenth-century call girl under the sponsorship of Comte
Jean-Baptiste du Barry. Louis XV made no secret that the
pleasure she gave him was "sensual enjoyment of an entirely
new sort." The Duc de Noailles surmised that this was because the royal lover had never visited a brothel.

Born Jeanne Bécu, of an unknown father and a servant
mother, she grew up to be a dazzling beauty whose star

57

quality was apparent to du Barry the moment he met her, a nineteen-year-old millinery apprentice already experienced in the ways of the *demimonde*. Du Barry, a gambler and well-known Parisian *roué*, installed her in his home, where she was soon known to his set as a good revenue producer through the employment of her special talents. But du Barry planned for greater conquests.

He altered Jeanne's name from Beauvarnier, her own invention, to Vaubernier, which both agreed had a more elegant ring to it, and schooled her to preside over the little suppers and *salons* that brought the racier members of French society under his roof. With du Barry's tutelage she honed her natural gifts and attractions into superb tools, and acquired a *savoir faire* that Madame de Pompadour had lacked in her early years.

Madame de Pompadour's place was exactly what du Barry had in mind for his protégée. To bring her to the king's attention, he one day stationed her in the forefront of a crowd gathered in the palace courtyard to watch the monarch pass. As they both had hoped, she caught the king's gaze. Louis's valet and occasional procurer, Lebel, was promptly dispatched to learn her identity.

With the king's interest aroused, du Barry settled down to serious planning. For Jean to fill the post of *maîtresse en titre*, vacant since Madame de Pompadour's death, she would need to be presented at court, with a titled husband in the background. Du Barry was unable to marry her himself because he already had a wife whom he had married for her fortune. The handiest alternative was to return the title of comte to his older brother, to whom it rightfully belonged in the first place, and then marry him to his protégée. This accomplished, the Comtesse du Barry was installed at Versailles.

There she met with the same stubborn resistance that Madame de Pompadour had received, but for different reasons. Despite her beauty and charm, she was regarded as little better than a professional courtesan by the court. Her vivacity and playfulness had attracted the king, but these very qualities weighed against her in the eyes of those who thought her lacking in respect for him. And his willing acceptance of her behavior in an age when majesty was treated with reverence and etiquette stood in place of religion, was considered equally shocking on his part. Evidently, within the hearing of others, she addressed him with the intimate *toi*, called him by her nickname for him, *La France*, and often used street language to amuse him.

One incident that has come to be known as the story of the coffee pot found its way into the accounts of many French historians reporting on the reign of Louis XV. At the little intimate *soupers* which he continued to enjoy with Madame du Barry as he had with Madame de Pompadour, he continued often to prepare their coffee. Once, when the coffee boiled over, Madame du Barry was heard to exclaim. *"La France, prends donc garde. Ton café fout le camp!'* The expression *fout le camp,* roughly meaning something out of control, was considered extremely vulgar, a phrase men might use in male company.

As official mistress, Madame du Barry did not meddle in affairs of state as Madame de Pompadour had often done. She did, however, manage to have the king's chief minister, Choiseul, exiled from court for his open dislike of her. Choiseul's departure might have impoverished the quality of court life. His extravagance and polished taste had set an example for others to strive toward. He had shaped and guided Madame de Pompadour's superb taste and been her good friend and mentor over the years. But Madame du Barry was not to be outdone by a dead predecessor. She had already learned the tastes and ways of elegant society in her days with du Barry and easily maintained the luxurious ambience that had surrounded Madame de Pompadour. Often she exceeded it. At Louveciennes, the lovely château presented to her by Louis XV, she substituted lapis lazuli for the marble fireplace facings. The guests who attended her receptions in the mirrored salon, lit with a thousand candles, danced on floors of rarest woods brought there by her order.

The dinners she served were always magnificent but never heavy. To make sure that everything was light, digestible, and extremely palatable, she employed a female cook for a while, responding to another new trend.

The preference for male cooks was gradually reversing. In 1782 Mercier could already see the change. "Some people prefer female cooks. They say that men cooks have their palate destroyed by the time they are forty." Women cooks were now as well trained as *chefs de cuisine.*

Cordon bleu, the title indicating the professionalism of female cooks, is said to have originated through the intercession of Madame du Barry. It may be legend, but supposedly mistress and king had indulged in a good-natured argument about the relative merits of the two sexes as cooks. Du Barry, with a female chef in her employ at the time and mindful of her mother's skill, offered to prove the superiority of women in the kitchen. The menu of the dinner her *cuisinière* prepared has been quoted many times in the two hundred years since it was served to Louis XV, and it remains a classic example of balance and exquisite taste:

Coulis de faisan
Clear pheasant consomme
Petites croustades de foie de lottes
Pastry cases filled with livers of burbot (a fresh-water fish)
Salmis de becassines
Ragout of snipe (a game bird)
Pain de volaille à la suprême
Molded, poached chicken forcemeat with sauce suprême
Poulard au cresson
Roast chicken garnished with watercress
Ecrevisses au vin de sauterne
Crayfish cooked in sauterne wine
Biscuit de pêche au noyau
An ice made of peaches and garnished with the edible seeds
of the pits
Crème de cerneaux
Liqueur made of green walnuts
Fraises au marasquin
Strawberries in maraschino

After the dinner the king is said to have acknowledged the *cuisinière's* superiority and Madame du Barry to have asked that she be granted the order of the *cordon bleu*. We may give some credence to this tale: evidently there was at the time a feminist movement to honor women with decorations and emblematic *cordons,* of which the *cordon bleu* was the highest. This brought a snappish outburst from Mercier, who wrote, "It has been proposed that women receive Orders and Cordons when their husbands are so honored. Perfectly ridiculous! The queen herself was not decorated. And what canoness has a *cordon bleu?*"

It is not known whether Louis XV granted Madame du Barry's request, but *cordon bleu* soon became the female alternative for *chef de cuisine.* However, Lady Sydney Morgan, the nineteenth-century Irish memoirist, wrote that the title of *cordon bleu* was first awarded to the *cuisinière* of the senior Grimod de la Reynière, father of the noted gastronome.

Madame du Barry's female chef is nameless, but a male chef, Salanave, who served her during the reign of Louis XVI and was dismissed for stealing, was to earn a dubious footnote in history for malice to a kind mistress, when his testimony to the Terror brought her to the guillotine.

After the death of Louis XV, Madame du Barry retired to Louveciennes to live a dignified country life. She was not welcome at the court because Marie Antoinette disliked her. By all accounts the former mistress was quite content to be quit of Versailles and now exhibited a marked preference for intellectual society rather than the frivolous. The Duc de Croy, visiting her, found her "still lovely and with a finer tone than one might have expected . . . it was difficult to persuade oneself of her former condition in life."

Her preference for country life was shared by many others of wealth and position. Arthur Young, in his sedulous account of travels through France in 1789, commented, "The present fashion in France for spending time in the country is new . . . Everybody having country seats is at them and those who have not, visit others who have . . . This revolution in French manners [is] one of the best features they have taken from England."

This "revolution" was part of the change that had come over court life with Louis XVI on the throne.

Come What May, Frenchmen Dine

"Dear friends should never long
abstain from feasts, For e'en
the memory of them is delightful."

Athenaeus

T he mantle of royalty fitted Louis XVI like a
blacksmith's smock. Given a choice, he might
have preferred the latter to his ermined robe of state. A forge
stood handy in his apartment and he spent many hours at it
fashioning keys and clock parts. The pleasure this afforded
him was second only to the pleasure he took in hunting, the
only one of his inclinations that seemed to link him to his
Bourbon ancestors.

He lacked the regal arrogance of Louis XIV, the ambiva-
lence and self-indulgence of Louis XV, and he established a
milestone of sorts as the only Bourbon king who did not take
a mistress. Indeed he had no desire for one. His marital obligation, when he was finally able to perform it with the aid of
a circumcision after seven years of impotence, was merely a
dutiful procreative gesture. Marie Antoinette was more a sex-
ually frustrated young wife than a capricious, frivolous
queen.

In many ways her inclinations were like those of her husband. She disliked court etiquette and often rebelled at it. She preferred simple dress and discarded long trains except for ceremonial occasions, causing Madame Campan, one of her ladies-in-waiting, to remark that "at last a duchess could not be distinguished from an actress." Court ladies followed Marie Antoinette's preferences, besieging Madame Bertin, her milliner, for the same caps and feathers, and making high fashion of her simple preferences. She liked to walk about unattended, and the rustic pleasures of the Petit Trianon, where she played at being a country lass, were not so much pursuit of folly as an expression of a secret yearning.

With a king who had no wish to play the absolute monarch, and a queen who rejected the appendages and prescribed conduct of royalty, the galvanic force that had generated excitement at court in the past was lacking. Court life was tempered to the point where it cooled off completely.

Such actions as Louis XVI took on the throne he reluctantly occupied reflected his democratic inclinations and alarmed the nobility, threatening to reopen the sixteenth- and seventeenth-century ruptures between king and nobles. Louis XIV had throttled the fractious nobles with his absolute authority; now Louis XVI seemed likely to turn authority over to the people. It was enough to make the nobility shake in their boots. Eventually many of them would help to destroy this unlikely Bourbon king.

In one respect Louis XVI was a complete Bourbon: a gluttonous eater. At one sitting he could down a whole chicken, four mutton chops, six eggs, and a slice of ham, and then fill in any available corners of his stomach with salad and *entremets*. Frenchmen had marveled at the appetites of their kings before this, but in 1792 Louis's display of his prodigious appetite before the Tribunal of the Terror, when he sat there wolfing down huge quantities of food, turned more than one citizen against him. (François Gérard, then an aspiring young painter, recorded the scene on canvas, but it was later whisked out of sight and Gérard painted a kinder representation of the king in his final days.) What had been accepted, even admired, as regal conduct was now condemned as the behavior of a sovereign pig. There were rumors that the royal family's attempted escape from France had failed because Louis had insisted on stopping to eat.

Louis XVI's table had offered no inspiration to the culinary arts. But the same had been true of the table of Louis XIV. Nevertheless, in both reigns gastronomy proceeded and expanded, propelled by a basic national characteristic exemplified in a remark by Chateaubriand: "At German and English tables, people eat—but they don't dine." Frenchmen dined. They continued to, as best they could, during the bleakest times.

The Revolution did not suddenly halt social life and dining pleasure. *Salons* continued to be held in the homes of Madame de Gondorcet and the Marquise de Chabonas where the literati mingled. Madame de Genlis played hostess to the Orleanists who hoped to emerge victorious over the house of Bourbon when the Revolution subsided. Madame Necker continued her intimate *soupers* on Tuesdays, offering a tempting table to such luminaries as Madame de Staël and Talleyrand.

Talleyrand, not yet a prince, was already a noted gastronome, along with the Comte de Barras, the Duc de Cambacérès, and Grimod de la Reynière. These men predicted the future of French cuisine at the tables they set before the Revolution and reluctantly abandoned through its duration.

Many Frenchmen continued to dine on their accustomed scale until crop failures due to droughts in 1793, 1794, and particularly 1795 created food shortages. Still, to judge from diary entries by a petit bourgeois Paris housewife, some tables enjoyed abundance despite this. What she served to fellow Republicans and labeled "a very poor meal," was meager only by comparison with the lavishness of earlier, less threatening times. "A first course of soup and a ham omelette; a second course of brisket of mutton, turnips, potatoes and cheese." The same chronicler recorded a more abundant meal, eaten as a guest in a friend's home, where the first course offered "soup, cold beef garnished with tiny pickles, beetroot salad; a second course of two kinds of fish sautéed in butter, stewed mutton with potatoes, several kinds of cheese, fruits and conserves." On still another occasion, picnicking in the country with friends, the family ate "meat pie, an enormous *pâté de maison*, baked cod with potatoes, salad, gingerbread, apples, and cheese." All these meals included wine, liqueurs, and coffee as a matter of course, and also a food new to French tables—the potato.

The French had avoided the nutritious white potato for many years because of its botanical connection with the deadly-nightshade family. Earlier, in the face of frequent threats of crop failure, Antoine-Auguste Parmentier, an agronomist, had decided that it was time to dispense with this groundless fear, which rightfully applied only to the plant's foliage. In 1774 he began a campaign to popularize this gift from the New World which had long been enjoyed by other European nations, especially England. By 1789, when the Revolution began, the potato was at home on most French tables, often in the form of bread. Parmentier had shown that it could be dried and reduced to flour.

Lalande, the astronomer, also experimented with untried aliments, but it is doubtful that many followed his urging to at least try such exotic tidbits as caterpillars and spiders to appease hunger pangs during food shortages. Caterpillars, he reported, tasted like almonds, spiders like nuts. Luckily, French cuisine has remained free of such invaders, though for years the snails relished by the French revolted other nationalities.

Paris continued to be the entry point for new additions to French cuisine, and as the Revolution accelerated, another gift from the New World arrived in the capital—the tomato. The romantic picture is that of patriotic French troops entering the city, singing the *Marseillaise* and bringing with them tomatoes from their native Provence. Troops there were; sing they did—a song that became known as the *Marseillaise*; and they did eat tomatoes, as many Mediterranean peoples did at that time, introduced to them by Spanish and Portuguese explorers. But these troops were actually hired assassins,

Talleyrand as he appeared during the ancien regime.

brought in by the newly formed and radical *Commune de Paris* to carry out the massacres of September 1792, when Paris gutters ran red with the blood of hundreds of political prisoners dragged from jails to be killed.

Blanc-Grilli, a Marseilles deputy to the Assembly in Paris, protested that they were not Frenchmen at all, but "a scum of criminals vomited out of the prisons of Genoa and Sicily . . . the dregs of all nations." They were recruited from among the unsavory toughs inhabiting the Marseilles waterfront, the *Marseillais*, as they were called; hence the name given to the song they adopted as their marching chant, which was actually *Chant de Guerre pour l'Armée du Rhin*, composed in Strasbourg by Rouget de Lisle for the French Army of the Rhine.

The strutting, singing mercenaries engaged the city's attention, but Parisians were either unaware of or curiously numb to their atrocities, and equally so to threats of an invasion by Austrian troops, rumored to be marching on the city. John Moore, an Englishman living in Paris in 1792, described the carnival spirit that swept the unconcerned city. "The Champs Elysées were crowded with strollers of one sort or another . . . booths were erected where refreshments were sold . . . music and dancing resounded . . . pantomimes and puppet shows were exhibited and . . . people were dancing."

Parisians continued to be unmoved when the Terror became a public spectacle, its victims chopped like so much poultry under the Italian refinement Dr. Guillotin had recommended to the Revolutionary Tribunal as more humane than torture, and quicker by far. The outside world looked on in horror, but Parisians were too close to the scene.

Those Frenchmen who were not politically active submitted to a few minor adjustments and led their normal lives during the Revolution. They addressed each other as "citizen" and "citizeness;" accepted an altered calendar; avoided contact with anyone likely to come under the scrutiny of the Terror; and ate rather well, all things considered.

As did the leaders of the Revolution. At table Revolutionaries were Frenchmen first, and Frenchmen dined. Louis Nicolardot, the French social historian, called the meals of the leading Revolutionaries "as delicate and delicious as those of the most famous gourmands." Danton, who with Robespierre and Marat switched the Revolution onto its bloody track, put "delicate food and exquisite wine" above all other joys, including beautiful women, as the ultimate prize of power attained.

Robespierre was known to carry eating to excess, especially if oranges were on the table—which they usually were, to gratify his insatiable appetite for them. When he dined with fellow Revolutionaries in a private dining room at the Café de Foy, he would slice the fruit on a miniature guillotine that served as a table centerpiece. If the group had drunk too freely, which was often the case, they indulged their macabre humor by decapitating a live chicken at the end of the meal.

Even in the imminence of the guillotine, Frenchmen still strove to dine. When victims of the Terror were carted off to prison where their fate soon became clear enough, many still retained this spirit and were determined to improve on prison fare to the best of their talents and resources. Some prisoners banded together to share their food and its preparation.

Madame Roland, who perished on the scaffold with the outraged cry, "O liberty, what crimes are committed in thy name!" belonged to such a group in La Force prison. It included the Comte de Kersaint, naval expert and distinguished host, who went to his cell followed by a battery of cooking utensils. His reputation as a host continued undiminished in La Force, where, Madame Roland reported, "When it was his turn [to plan the meal] we always knew it would be the most dainty and abundant."

In jail or out, few minds were easy during the Terror. Banker, lawyer, noble, chef—if their sympathies or connections were at all suspect, they were safer out of France when the Jacobins came to power. Prudent Frenchmen heeded the ominous clouds before the downpour began. Many who did not, or could not, get away quickly enough, or who hoped to gain by their action, turned on former friends, masters, and relatives. The Duke d'Orléans, who voted for the death of

Louis XVI, hoping for the restoration of a monarchy favorable to his house, was the most notorious. Salanave, chef to Madame du Barry, was one of the meanest.

Many accomplished chefs, fearful of running afoul of the Terror, followed their employers into self-imposed exile or found new posts in other countries. Louis Ude, when no longer needed in the kitchens of Louis XVI, fled to England, where he brought royal splendor to the tables of the Duke of York and the Earl of Sefton. When the Duke of York died, Ude mourned in reverse, "O my good Duke. How you will miss me where you have gone!" He remained in England and shared his versatile talents in his book, *The French Cook*, teaching the English how to make his *Riz verte, Blanquette du poulet Marbrée* (chicken and tongue) and *Longe de veau en surprise*.

Those chefs who returned when the Terror ended were welcomed back by eager gastronomes longing to have their tables restored, to taste once again what Talleyrand described as "the sweetness of life of the *ancien régime*." One of the best known of these gastronomes was the Comte de Barras, a renowned host before the Revolution and an active participant in it from its start, through the Terror, to the Directory (1795), the Consulate (1799), and finally the Empire in 1804.

As a leader of the Directory, he boosted the obscure young General Bonaparte on his quick climb to power as First Consul and then Emperor.

Barras's activities as a host tapered off during the Revolution, but he impatiently resumed them as soon as it seemed safe to do so. The mopping up after the Terror was still in progress when he gave a small dinner for twelve, as interesting for its timing and some of its guests as for its menu. Among the guests were the Deputy Tallien, who led the insurrection against Robespierre; Tallien's lovely wife, Thérésa; and Josephine Beauharnais, Barras's mistress of the moment whom he was soon to marry off to Napoleon.

The day after the dinner, May 20, 1795, riots broke out in Paris against the Revolutionary Convention, where a struggle for leadership was being waged, with Barras, Tallien, and their cohorts ranged against another faction. Three days later order had been restored and six deputies who had supported the insurgent rioters were quickly condemned and hurried off to execution. Had the dinner been a precelebration of an engineered confrontation that would remove the opposition? Or was it merely a pleasant gathering of Barras's intimates? Whatever its purpose, every detail of the dinner itself was planned to perfection.

It began with a rich onion soup and a *relève* of roast sturgeon, followed by a well-conceived second course of six entrées, two roasts, and six *entremets,* and concluded with twenty-four desserts, presumably portions and not varieties. Ices were served midway in the meal as a refresher. Here is Barras's menu:

Potage aux petits oignons
Onion soup
Troncon d'esturgeon à la broche
Large piece of sturgeon roasted on a spit

Les Six Entrées
Sauté de filets de turbot
Filets of turbot, sautéed
Anguilles à la tartare
Eel with tartar sauce
Concombres farcis à la moelle
Cucumbers stuffed with marrow
Vol-au-vent blanc de volaille à la Béchamel
vol-au-vent filled with diced chicken breast in Béchamel sauce
St. Pierre aux câpres
A European fish, John Dory in English, served with capers
Filets de perdrix en anneaux
Partridge filets arranged in a ring

Les Deux Plats de Rôti
Goujons de departement
Small fresh-water fish of the region
Carpe au court-bouillon
Carp poached in bouillon

Les Six Entremets
D'œufs à la neige
Eggs in snow, also known as floating island
Betteraves blanches sautés au jambon
Beets, slightly cooked, then sautéed with strips of ham
Gelée au vin de Madère
Madeira wine jelly
Beignets de crème à la fleur d'oranges
Fritters with chilled, orange-flavored custard
Lentilles à la crème au blond de veau
Lentils in a hot cream sauce
Culs d'artichauts à la ravigote
Artichoke bottoms in a hot, spicy white sauce
Salade céleri en rémoulade
Cooked celery stalks, chilled and sauced with mayonnaise
containing various green herbs, minced onions and minced
pickles

For his feast Barras ordered cushions placed on the chairs of
the ladies, and sternly specified, "Get the ices from Veloni. I
will have no others." This was the veritable host speaking,
determined to have only the best at his table and able to instruct his staff to that end.

Soon Barras would be rejoined by such noted hosts as Talleyrand and Cambacérès, whose tables had endowed the *ancien régime* with some of its luster. Like Barras, Talleyrand and
Cambacérès were of the nobility and had survived the Revolution while actively participating in it. Wily politicians with
reptilian agility and instincts to match, all three men were
loyal to whomever and whatever would benefit them. Their
ultimate goal was the protection of their pleasures and
luxuries, the exquisite table foremost among them.

Together with a prankish gourmand, Grimod de la
Reynière, they would lead the renaissance of the host, or amphitryon, as he would now call himself, and these amphitryons would again enlarge French cuisine.

Barras at the time of the Revolution.

The Age of Carême

Grimod de la Reynière in late life. From Les Classiques de la Table.

Host Into
Amphitryon

*"A warmed up dinner was
never worth anything."*

Nicolas Boileau

The Revolution leveled Frenchmen like a scythe swinging through tall grass; social boundaries disappeared like dismantled fences in its path. By the time of the Consulate the leveling was nearly complete. The nouveaux riches, many with purses enlarged by profits from the wars Napoleon was waging, thronged drawing rooms that formerly would have been closed to them. Nobles who had fled the Revolution as *émigrés* and had returned to a penniless existence found themselves on the same social footing with *commissaries* who sold provisions and goods to the army. Men who had previously lived precariously by bartering were now princes of finance.

It was the day of the self-made man who knew how to turn a franc to profit. France had known many of this breed in the past, but never in such numbers, and never before so aggressively eager to elevate themselves socially and to enjoy the life of the privileged. It was as if these newcomers to

77

wealth feared that the riches they held in their hands might disappear in a moment—a reasonable fear considering the political and economic uncertainties that followed the Terror.

But fears aside, even if the future seemed unclouded, it was good business for a man to present the evidence of his success to the world. Riches, renown, and titles had come to those who knew how to spend their money conspicuously, as the sixteenth-century magnate Samuel Bernard had demonstrated by spending fortunes on his table, living in a style that very nearly matched a king's. The Rothschilds would soon follow Bernard's example and were already profiting from the wars in which France was engaged.

Like Bernard, the newcomers to wealth sought to become renowned hosts. The *bonne chère* that every Frenchman of reasonable means enjoyed—good fare prepared by his wife with perhaps the aid of a maid-servant, for guests who were family friends—was inadequate for a financier who wanted to be a host in the grand manner.

With Napoleonic France in the grip of the classic age— ladies arraying themselves in diaphanous Grecian draperies, children baptized Hercule, Achille, and Lycurgus—it was natural for the host to acquire an identity consistent with the times. He became an amphitryon.

In the comic tale by Plautus, Amphitryon's wife was seduced by Jupiter, disguised as her husband. When the two Amphitryons confronted each other, the witnesses present could not determine the real one. But when Jupiter grandly invited them into Amphitryon's house to dine, as if it were his home, even Amphitryon's devoted servant, Sosia, unable to recognize his master otherwise, was sure that only Amphitryon would play the host. Mistakenly pointing to Jupiter, he cried, "His words end all uncertainty; the true Amphitryon is he who serves us dinner."

The choice of Amphitryon to replace the honorable title of host seems strained, and exactly who was responsible for the transmutation of cuckold into quintessential host is uncertain. But a good guess points to the literate gastronome Grimod de la Reynière, self-appointed savior of French gastronomy after the Revolution, in whose *Almanach des Gour-*

mands the new synonym for host appears for the first time. Not just any host, mind you. Amphitryon was meant to describe the *knowledgeable* host who took his responsibilities seriously. For Grimod de la Reynière, no other kind was worth discussing.

If Grimod de la Reynière meant the choice of word to be a prank, he was just the man to do it, and the time was ripe. Practical jokes and amusing tricks called "mystifications" were the rage at that time. Professional jokesters were available for hire. Grimod himself is said to have made his elegant country home into a "fun house" like those in amusement parks, with unexpected trap doors, mysterious voices, and ancestral portraits that suddenly jutted out tongues at startled guests.

A representation of Grimod de la Reynière's "funeral" dinner.

Grimod was an old hand at such antics. Before the Revolution, when his renown as a host vied with his notoriety as a prankster, his most famous dinner was staged for friends who came to attend his funeral. Announcement of the obsequies, sent to friends after his two-week feigned illness, caused mutterings about the inconvenient hour set for the service, the hour when upper-class French folk usually supped. When Grimod appeared, lively as a cricket, and opened the doors to the dining salon where a crêpe-covered table bore a magnificent feast, they were overjoyed. To cap the evening, the guests were conveyed home in hearses.

Grimod de la Reynière was born into a family of wealth, where the silver spoon of fortunate birth was shared even by the horses; they fed from silver troughs. Unhappily, Grimod's birth was not totally fortunate. He was born with a cruel deformity: stumps instead of hands. His father sought the most expert aid in Switzerland and equipped his son with remarkable prostheses that enabled him to eat dextrously and to handle a paint brush skillfully.

Grimod rewarded his concerned parent with scant gratitude. On one occasion he made him the butt of a hilarious dinner by dressing a live pig in the absent father's uniform of *fermier general* and seating the porker in the host's chair to greet the guests. The symbolism was appropriate enough. The *fermiers general* were official tax collectors for the king, gougers of the worst order, and considered "pigs" by all taxpayers.

Grimod's pranks ceased when the Revolution began. His more serious pursuits as writer, editor, and occasional drama critic were also halted while he sat out the Terror quietly in the home of an aunt in the South of France, managing to excape involvement in the Revolution.

When he did reappear to indulge his wit and appetite in the company of friends, the Consulate had begun. Social life had resumed its former pace. One might have thought the *ancien régime* still existed. Balls, dinners, and a festive spirit animated the sphere of the wealthy, but a closer look revealed that the participants had changed. To some recently returned

Frenchmen who had formerly dwelt at the top of society, the changes were shocking, particularly in public places. James Forbes, an Englishman detained in France when war was declared between the two countries during the Consulate, repeated what one repatriate had said after visiting the theater: "The boxes were filled with shameless women, infamous contractors and *commissaries*, making an indecent parade of their lewd acquisitions and cruel spoils, and insulting the public misery by their shameful and disgusting luxury."

This new society did not annoy Grimod de la Reynière. He had recently inherited his father's fortune, kept intact during the Revolution by the machinations of his astute parent. Why should he begrudge any man his new money? Instead, in this shift of fortune Grimod saw a new *raison d'être:* he would aid the newcomers to become amphitryons. Like the master of the hunt he sounded the call, "For a rich man the most beautiful role in the world is to be an amphitryon."

It was one thing to yearn to be one; to succeed was another matter. Just as Barras had known where to procure the finest

Grimod de la Reynière's jury de gustateurs *in session. Frontispiece of* L'Almanach des Gourmands, *1805.*

ices for his guests, so the untutored needed to know where to obtain the finest *pâtisserie*, the smoothest pâtés, and the most exquisite *friandises*.

As a first step Grimod conceived the *Almanach des Gourmands* in 1803, and continued to publish it annually until 1812. In it he discussed various foods, especially those in season or suitable to the time of year. He also recommended suppliers. Some accused him of bias in his recommendations, but surely he acted without guile when he put in a word for the English table by recommending beef, prepared English style, for December's bracing weather. "What the English call beefsteak, cut thin, briefly grilled, seasoned only with salt and pepper and served on a hot plate. It is their principal dish and deserves a Channel crossing to savor. Few of our ragouts can compare to beef used this way."

Tomatoes, so recently introduced to Parisians, were now grown in hothouses (as were berries and other out-of-season delights) and available in December. "This vegetable or fruit, however you wish to call it, was very expensive when first introduced to Paris during the Revolution," he explained. "Now you can find it heaped in baskets at Les Halles, reasonably priced." He raved about its properties. "It gives delicious flavor to the most mediocre dishes . . . is unsurpassable for sauces . . . in soups . . . and what a delicious *entremet* it makes. Try it," he urged, "seeded, cooked with some sausage, parsley, onions, chopped tarragon, a touch of garlic, and crowned with lemon juice just before serving." His descriptions were worthy of modern food writers. "No matter how much of this you serve, it is never enough," he promised.

Whenever some new culinary idea presented itself, in a restaurant or at a friend's table, Grimod was quick to share it with his readers. A potage devised by his friend M. Camerani of the Opera-Comique was promptly baptized *potage Camerani* by Grimod. It combined macaroni, or more probably spaghetti (all pastas were still *maccaroni* to the French), with chicken livers and Parmesan cheese—the likely ancestor of spaghetti Caruso. *Salade de volaille* (with the meat left on the bone), surrounded by shredded lettuce forming nests for anchovies and cornichons, intrigued him, as did a cold cherry soup, *Soupe aux cerises*, "little known in Paris as yet."

Highest praise was heaped on *Fanchons* and *Fanchonettes*, "the most exquisite pastry imaginable, requiring long experience and profound knowledge of the art of pastry making." If an amphitryon's chef was not equal to the task, the pastries could be procured in the shop of their creator, M. Rouget, who had been inspired to make them by the performance of the actress Mme. Henri-Belmont in the play *Fanchon*.

Grimod took his readers on a descriptive tour of the various shops he considered worthy of notice, but in the famous Palais Royal, "among the numerous marchands de comestibles . . . which multiply daily," there were only three worth discussing. In one, a "remarkable pyramidal display intermingled pâtés of every sort with liqueurs, vinegars, mustards, stuffed tongues and stuffed turkeys, raw and cooked truffles, and lobsters." In another temple of eatables "The most blasé gourmand will be moved. What is displayed would fill an encyclopedia, in categories alone; as for types in these categories—" words failed Grimod and he advised the amphitryon to "carefully study everything shown."

The suppliers recommended in the *Almanach* were chosen by a *Jury de Gustateurs* organized by Grimod from among his friends in the arts and included former members of the Wednesday Society, a group of gastronomes that had disbanded during the Revolution.

Nine of the sixteen jurors were women, including Mme. Henri-Belmont, the star of *Fanchon*. "But it was difficult to get this jury in skirts to observe the punctuality so foreign to their nature," observed a biographer of Grimod. Grimod coped with the problem by imposing fines for tardiness. Mademoiselle Mézeray, who committed a more serious infraction by absenting herself from a meeting on the pretext of illness, only to be seen that same evening at the opera in superb health, received a Draconian punishment: banishment from all jury meetings for three years.

Generally, though, Grimod was kindly disposed to women, as gastronomes—after all he accepted them as jurors—and as cooks. His own kitchen was in the hands of a tyrannical *cordon bleu*, Hélène, who gave him twenty-five years of exalted dining.

In 1807 Grimod de la Reynière published a more elaborate work to guide his flock—*Manuel des Amphitryons*. It covered everything an amphitryon needed to know for the management of a distinguished table and warned those who lived in the country not to extend invitations too freely to city dwellers, "or you will be running a hotel." Menus were supplied, planned according to the season, time of day, and number of guests to be served. They were not for amphitryons of modest means, but as Grimod pointed out, "Money alone does not make an excellent table." The contest was open to any host with imagination and the will to insist on variety and quality.

Table deportment was covered, with some pertinent remarks for guests as well. For those making their first forays into gourmand society: "If you don't want to be mistaken for a Huron and make your host blush, you must learn correct behavior." Management of the napkin was vital. It was not to be worn around the neck, but fastened into a buttonhole and allowed to drape over the knees. Fear that sauce might drip on shirt or cravat was dismissed as unworthy of a guest with a sense of responsibility to his host; correct deportment was a guest's first obligation.

Only a spoon entered a soup plate; never a fork. If vegetables or whatever else the soup contained were oversize, well,

A gastronome's dream. Frontispiece of L'Almanach des Gourmands, *1808.*

too bad; the diner would need to use his ingenuity, but no fork. When the spoon had done its work it was to be placed on the plate, carefully. No dripping allowed on the tablecloth. If the guest was behind the times and didn't know that the *rince-bouche* was no longer fashionable (a bowl-like glass from which a diner could take a sip of water, swirl it in his mouth, and squirt it back into the glass) he could ask for one and the host would have it brought. But, Grimod reminded him, it was distinctly passé in 1807. Perhaps the worst breach, *"une grande incongruité,"* was to cut one's bread with a knife. It must be broken by hand.

It was proper to pass servings to nearby neighbors, always bearing in mind that a *gourmand* should not receive a portion suitable for a *maîtresse*. If ladies were present at the table they could assist the service by piling biscuits and macaroons on a plate to pass around. "Ladies always serve *le désert* beautifully," said Grimod. "It is a pleasure to watch their dextrous white hands in motion."

One third of the *Manuel* dealt with carving, an important function of the polished amphitryon. Precise illustrations of various fowl, meats, and fish, with the path of each incision charted and numbered, made it possible for even a novice carver to perform skillfully. Large joints and roasts were best carved by the *maître d'* or official carver, if the staff included one, at a side table, and then passed to the guests by servitors.

That noted host the Prince de Cambacérès, Second Consul during the Consulate and Archchancellor during the Empire, preferred to do *all* the carving himself, which may have been the reason some meals at his table went on for five hours. A guest at a dinner for thirty-six spoke of the many butlers in attendance, but remarked that Cambacérès did all the carving, consulting each guest as to his preference, while brandishing tidbits on his fork. He professed to do this in the interest of hospitality, but some detractors, Carême among them, gossiped that in this way he maintained a kind of portion control.

Cambacérès was said to review the leftovers of each meal

after the guests had departed. If there were enough he planned a menu around them for the next day. This was permissible in an ordinary household. But in the home of an amphitryon? Never.

However, there were others who maintained tight control over the larder. That most noted gastronome Frederick the Great regularly inspected the bills for provisions and knew, down to the last pit, how many cherries had been eaten. The Countess Potocka once slipped into his study and found a plate of the fruit on the king's desk with a warning note alongside, "I leave eighteen."

Gossip about the table of Cambacérès was second only to gossip about his preference for male companions. He made no secret of it, according to rumors at the time he became Second Consul. "I visit chippies like everyone else," he said. "And when I'm finished I say, 'Adieu messieurs.'" Once, late for a meeting with Napoleon, he offered the excuse that a fair visitor had delayed him. Napoleon, retorted, "Next time when I await you, have the goodness to say to this lady, 'Take your hat and cane and go'!"

Napoleon, who could dispatch an entire meal in fifteen minutes and often did, had as little feeling for gourmandise as a hod carrier, but he knew its importance to nineteenth-century statecraft. Cambacérès' ability to manage both pleased him. At the Congress of Luneville he gave Cambacérès' table the sanction of official business. "You know the table is important in diplomacy," Cambacérès wailed to the *chargé d'affaires* when an order banned the use of the official dispatch box for anything but official business, "How can one make friends without serving choice food?" Napoleon heard of the affair and assured the distraught amphitryon, "The couriers will continue to bring your truffled turkeys, Mayence pastries, and red-legged partridges."

Napoleon did not engage in the dinner-table diplomacy he urged on Cambacérès and Talleyrand. He was ruled by an almost irrational desire to finish each meal as quickly as possible. Whether he ate alone or was host at a state banquet, he bolted his food. The pace he set was impossible for most diners to match, and no matter who the guests, or what the occasion or number at table, when his hunger was satisfied, he rose, obliging all others to do likewise. Entire meals were often left unfinished.

With the noted chef Dunand preparing the food, under the guidance of the equally noted *maître d'hôtel* Louis de Cussy, guests at Napoleon's table must have known the tortures of Tantalus. Few managed to savor even a fraction of what was presented, especially if not forewarned. Madame Divov, wife of a Russian diplomat, had not been, and the invitation that had "thrilled" her when it arrived became memorable as a frustrating experience. "A state dinner that was over in less than an hour!" she reported indignantly. The usual time would have been at least three hours.

That this speed was indeed usual at Napoleon's table was confirmed by Madame de la Tour du Pin in her memoirs. "We were at dinner for less than three-quarters of an hour," she wrote, but for her "that dinner is one of the events I remember with the most pleasure." The company included the king and queen of Westphalia, the Empress Marie Louise, other coroneted heads, "and myself on the Emperor's left. He spoke to me nearly all the time, of materials, laces . . . monuments, antiquities." The nectar of flattering attention obviously satisfied Madame de la Tour du Pin's appetite.

Despite his ungracious conduct as a host, Napoleon would not tolerate it in others who moved in court circles. He expected them to entertain graciously and frequently, as part of his determined effort to make the French court as brilliant as it had been in the days of the Bourbons when Soubise, Condé, Rochefoucauld, and others dazzled the court with sumptuous fêtes.

The task now devolved on less princely shoulders. Many of Napoleon's officials "were not out of the top drawer," as one disdainful historian put it, but Napoleon quickly remedied such inequities of birth by creating a new nobility of a thousand barons, four hundred counts, thirty-two dukes, and three princes, one of the three being his brother-in-law, General Murat. Murat, born the son of an innkeeper, quickly adjusted to the status of prince and fancied himself the counterpart of the great Condé of Louis XIV's reign. As a soldier the preening, insufferable general was not even a pale shadow of that great warrior, but he matched Condé's reputation as a host by bagging the noted chef Laguipière. With Laguipière in his kitchen, Murat gave formidable competition to such reigning amphitryons as Cambacérès and Talleyrand. When Napoleon, who handed his relatives kingdoms and titles like so many sweetmeats, made Murat king of Naples, Laguipière followed him there and later accompanied him on the Russian campaign. The great chef froze to death on the retreat from Moscow, leaving only hearsay accounts of his accomplishments, and no recorded recipes.

Napoleon's sister Pauline, a princess with a venerable title by her marriage to Prince Camille Borghese of the ancient Roman house, compensated for her brother's failings as a host by making the Borghese balls central to the social life of the First Empire.

The competitive spirit of the Bourbon days returned to social life. Those who now controlled the power and finances of France asserted their wealth and importance with large staffs and sumptuous tables, but the magnitude of an entertainment could sometimes strain the capacity even of a *grande* kitchen. At such times kitchen staffs were supplemented by extra help. These "hands" might be supplied by a catering establishment, along with food prepared there, or be specialists in their fields—pastries, roasts, *entremets*, and the like—who made a full-time profession of part-time work, or privately employed chefs who hired out as "extras" on their days off. A visiting ambassador or prince could put together an entire staff, complete from *maître d'* to scullions, for a stay of a few days or a residence of months. Alexander of Russia and other Allied leaders quartered in Paris at the end of Napoleon's reign assembled their staffs in this way.

Pastry chefs were the most in demand of all the specialists. Those who could execute superior *pièces montées*, the lavish pastry structures that decorated the center of the banquet table, were competed for like well-dowered brides.

Around 1805 the exceptional creations of a young chef employed in the Pâtisserie Bailly caught the attention of Talleyrand or of Talleyrand's chef and was told he would be welcome as an extra when the Archchancellor entertained. Young Marie-Antoine Carême soon became a frequent extra in the Talleyrand establishment. Eventually he shortened Marie-Antoine to Antonin and joined the select group of chefs who served whomever they pleased for as long as they pleased, and it pleased Carême to serve Talleyrand, off and on, for ten years.

Thus began a career dedicated to the true amphitryon. It carried French cuisine to a new summit.

CUISINE
ARTISTIQUE

A Pastry Cook
Presents the
Grande Cuisine

*"Dinners cannot be long
where dainties want."*

John Heywood

A ppraising Antonin Carême stirs up a mixture of admiration for his talent and annoyance with the qualities that earned him many detractors. He was boastful as a Gascon, conceited as a coxcomb, and a pretentious writer. But he was a truly talented artist who introduced many important innovations and systematized the *grande cuisine* of France. His immense contribution to gastronomy is undeniable. In the end admiration wins.

It seems fitting to meet him at the height of his accomplishments, in the home of his last employer, Baron James de Rothschild. So let us join the vivacious wit Lady Sydney Morgan on a visit to the Rothschild home, and at the same time glimpse the mode of life attained by newcomers to wealth and title, as viewed through eyes well accustomed to such surroundings.

Lady Morgan was receiving "two noted amphitryons when a dinner invitation was brought in from Monsieur and

Carême. Portrait in his L'Art de la Cuisine Francaise, *volume I.*

Madame de Rothschild." She read it aloud to her guests and was complimented on her luck. "You are going to dine at the first table in France—In Europe," the envious amphitryons told her. "You are going to judge from your personal experience, of the genius of Carême."

No ordinary genius, this Carême, her guests assured her. He lived in the style of the wealthy hosts he served. "Anecdotes beyond number were then given of the pomps and vanities of the life of Carême; the number of aides attached to his staff; his box at the opera, and other proofs of sumptuosity and taste, which . . . increased my desire to make his acquaintance."

Off went Lady Morgan "on a lovely July evening" to the Rothschild villa, Château de Boulogne, on the outskirts of Paris. "From the moment that the gates of the domain were thrown open . . ." she continues, "we found ourselves enclosed within a paradise . . . Flowers of all regions, fruits of all climes, tropical birds, English verdure . . . delicious music . . . were the preludes to admission into that salon, where we found the lady of the enchanted palace . . . [and] a large society of distinguished persons."

"The dining room stood apart from the house in the midst of orange trees . . . an elegant oblong pavilion of Grecian marble, refreshed by fountains . . . Porcelain beyond the price of all precious metals . . . consorted with . . . the sumptuous simplicity which reigned over the whole."

Of the meal itself she wrote, "Distillations of the most delicate viands . . . Every meat presented its own natural aroma; every vegetable its own shade of verdure. The *mayonese* was fried in ice [intensely cold] . . . the tempered chill of the *plombière* [a fruit ice of nectarines] satisfied every sense . . . With less genius than went into the composition of this dinner, men have written epic poems."

No feast under Carême's direction lacked one of his spectacular *pièces montées*. This time, to the delight of Lady Morgan, the lavish creation complimented her. It was "a column of the most ingenious confectionery architecture, on which my name was inscribed in spun sugar. *My* name in sugar! . . . I begged to be introduced to the celebrated and flattering artist . . . a well-bred gentleman . . . and when we had mutually complimented each other on our respective works, he bowed himself out, and got into his carriage, which was waiting to take him to Paris."

Designs for pièces montées, *drawn by Carême for his first work, Le Patissier Royal Parisien, 1815.*

Lady Morgan's thoughts dwelt on the noted chef as she returned from the Rothschild dinner. Her entire account of the excursion into this monied realm is a statement about the new dynastic wealth and the waning power of kings.

"Nothing of the . . . story of Carême was unknown to me . . . [He] was sought by all the sovereigns of the Continent; and, like Titian, he refused some royal and some imperial invitations . . . It was his peculiar good fortune to find in France a service . . . worthy of his genius . . . chef of Monsieur le Baron Rothschild, at a salary well beyond what any sovereign in Europe might be able to pay, even though assisted by Monsieur Rothschild; without whose aid so many sovereigns would scarcely have been able to keep cooks at all."

Culinary inspiration no longer came only from kings or nobles. What such nineteenth-century hosts as the Rothschilds demanded from their master chefs (who had long since overcome their reluctance to work for the non-noble) often surpassed the tables of kings.

Lady Morgan's enthusiastic outpourings were written in 1829, four years before Carême's death. By then his reputation as an innovative chef was well established and he had produced four important works on culinary practices: *Le Pâtissier Royal Parisien* (1815); *Le Pâtissier Pittoresque* (1815); *Le Maître d'Hôtel Française* (1822); and *Le Cuisinier Parisien* (1828). His final work, the definitive five-volume *L'Art de la Cuisine au Dix-neuvième Siècle* was already under way.

Each book built solidly on its predecessors, and when *L'Art de la Cuisine Française* was finally finished, the *grande* or *haute* cuisine of France was codified down to the last petite sauce. Carême completed only three volumes before his death. The last two were completed by Armand Plumerey from Carême's notes.

An important innovation, detailed illustrations, appeared in Carême's first work, *Le Pâtissier Royal Parisien*. Before then such precise instruction was unknown in any culinary work. A hundred and forty-nine drawings showed elaborate *pièces montées*, ornamented *croustades* to use as serving dishes, *vol-*

au-vents, talmouses, and *croque-en-bouchées.* The drawings were done by Carême with superb draftsmanship. Even more impressive, he was self-taught. For years he had studied the architectural drawings of Palladio and Vignole. Detailed instructions explained every step of preparing and constructing the intricate creations he designed.

It would have been pleasing had he stood aside to wait for the applause, but modesty is a becoming adornment to success that few achievers choose to wear—Carême least of all. Most chefs who shared their knowledge approached the task with at least a pretense at humility. Not Carême. This first book opened with thirty-five pages of introduction, much of it devoted to proclaiming his talent. He acknowledged a debt to some chefs he had worked alongside: Murat's Laguipière, whom he venerated, Talleyrand's Boucher, and the pastry chef Avice.

Either he did not know, or he did not choose to acknowledge his contemporary, the restaurateur and chef Antoine Beauvilliers, who had just published *L'Art du Cuisinier* (1814), the first important French culinary work since 1755, when *Les Soupers de la Cour* introduced the rococo *cuisine moderne.*

Beauvilliers' two-volume work covered everything that was standard practice among professional chefs at that time. He included the basic sauces *grande velouté* and *espagnole,* and most of their offspring sauces. Carême would cover these later and add numerous variations. *L'Art du Cuisinier* appeared almost simultaneously with Carême's first book, which dealt only with pastry and sweet *entremets.* The cuisine was still referred to as *la cuisine moderne* in both books.

Each man spoke to a different audience. The separation of French cuisine into two streams, *haute* and *bourgeoise* (home cooking) is apparent. Though Carême included most basic French dishes, he managed to make their preparation sound formidably difficult. His works were meant for the homes of Talleyrands and Rothschilds. His indexes are alive with dishes bearing contemporary names: *à la Genlis, à la Victor Hugo, à la Rossini, à la Chateaubriant,* and *à la Rothschild,* possibly dishes he had concocted and dedicated to these celebrated personages. But this did not mean they were entirely original creations. Beauvilliers described how the same dish could wear ten different names.

"Someone like Laguipière, Dalegre, or Lenoir can add or subtract something from a well-known dish as a composer or decorator would, and give it a name *de fantasie*, or the name of his patron or employer. This new attribution gives a familiar dish the charm of novelty. The dish loses its *primitif* name and becomes known by the modern one. In this way cutlets garnished with *purée d'oignon* become *côtelettes à la Soubise*."

Beauvilliers kept to the *primitif* names, which naturally resulted in a slimmer culinary repertoire, but one better suited to the audience he had chosen to address. As he explained, "The many names which express the same idea confuse the student who wants to know how to properly prepare certain standard dishes. A housewife will be able to find in my book all known dishes and also those of my own invention."

Carême warned housewives away from his pages. "Bourgeois kitchens of limited means would be wise to follow simple methods and not try to imitate the ways of the *grandes*," he said sternly. Indeed, it was a sensible caution. What bourgeois kitchen would want to attempt *jambon braisé et farci à la Rothschild*? This opulent dish began with a simple braised ham, but after successive adornments it was no longer recognizable as a ham. First it was enveloped in a rich farce of pheasant breasts. Then, surmounting it at the center, a large rosette was constructed of overlapping pheasant breasts alternating with strips of truffles. The creation—it could no longer be called just a ham—was enthroned in a setting of Soubise sauce and surrounded with a ragoût of cocks' combs and cocks' kidneys, scallops of foie gras, and julienne strips of pickled tongue and mushrooms. As if this were not gilding enough, the chef d'oeuvre was crowned with ten *hâtelets* bearing cocks' combs and scallops of hare.

Ham à la Berchou, named for the author of the poem *La Gastronomie*, was prepared in the same way as *à la Rothschild*, but when its turn for concealment came it was hidden under a farce of chicken, then ornamented with crawfish tails and

truffles. It reposed in a vinaigrette sauce containing veal noisettes, mushrooms, cocks' combs, crawfish, and black truffles. One can only speculate as to how many cocks gave their combs to gastronomy.

Despite different *à la* attributions, *potages de Macaroni* were basically the same dish: successive, alternating layers of pasta, quenelles, and grated Parmesan cheese, differing only in the composition of the quenelles. For *à la Rossini* they were of partridge forcemeat; for *à la Numa*, quail forcemeat, and so it went. Carême managed to make even Soubise sauce—a simple purée of onions in Béchamel sauce—a complicated undertaking by giving two lengthy versions in which one used chicken broth while the other used milk. Though Caréme's intent was to aid professionals, at times he instructed them as if they were schoolboys.

But enough of cavil. Carême is a giant in gastronomy. He made the most of such scientific inventions as heat controls, invented by the American expatriate Benjamin Thompson, that now made it possible to closely regulate range and oven temperatures. And he may also have invented the modern way of making soufflés.

Carême arrived at success early and swiftly, driven at first by real hunger and needing to feed himself at an age when most children enter first grade, and later by the hunger for success. In 1791, when he was seven, a homeless lad supposedly turned out by a father who could no longer support his large brood, Carême found shelter and work in a cookshop. By 1801, the time of the Consulate, he had progressed from kitchen scullion through various jobs and employers to the pastry shop of M. Bailly, where he remained for several years and learned the basics of fine pastry making.

It was an auspicious time for a young pastry cook on his way to achieving the rank of *chef de cuisine*. Under the Consulate France had returned to normal, wealth was openly flaunted, and accomplished chefs were again at a premium. Entertaining on a grand scale was resumed when Napoleon became emperor, Talleyrand leading off with a revival of the magnificent fêtes that had made him a notable host of the *ancien régime*. For some observers Talleyrand's entertainments "really marked the renascence of Paris life."

The rebirth extended to less pretentious tables as well. The windows of the *pâtisseries* in the Palais Royal, Bailly's among them, displayed luscious examples of the pastry cook's art for any Parisians with the francs to buy them. Tarts glistened with dewy fruit, marzipan fantasies imitated the bounties of the garden, petit-fours bathed in fondant were decorated as exquisitely as pieces of Sèvres—the whole array posed against pyramids of sugared and glacéd almonds, marrons and fruits. *Socles* and *pièces montées* meant for the tables of the *grandes* invited the gaze of passers-by and showed to what heights pastry chefs carried their art when bidden.

Talleyrand's table was often supplemented with elaborate creations from Bailly's pâtisserie. Carême would accompany them to the Talleyrand palace and set them in place properly. This may have brought him to the attention of Talleyrand's chef, Boucheseiche, known as Bouche, following the common practice among artists in those days of choosing a cognomen. By this name he appears in Carême's pages as one of his early and most helpful mentors. It was a fortunate beginning.

Aspiring chefs needed to acquire knowledge and experience in every culinary department. This was a compelling reason for moving from one post to another, and for working as an extra under noted chefs at every opportunity. Carême followed this pattern. He remained with Bailly four years, then moved to the pastry shop of M. Gendron where he worked only part-time in order to have more time to study drawing and to work as an extra, frequently for Talleyrand.

When his reputation was established, Carême decided to organize the cuisine of his day into a master work and to conserve his energy for this purpose, working only when, and for whom, he chose. He was as selective as the earlier *maître-queux-porte-chappes*, refusing would-be employers if their standards did not suit him. Heaven help the parsimonious hosts who may have tried to hire him. Carême probably insulted them openly, as he did Cambacérès for using leftovers.

Most of his employment was temporary. His longest stay before he entered the Rothschild employ was two years with the future George IV of England. Carême boasted that his royal employer suffered few attacks of gout under his careful dietary supervision.

Carême professed to have left him because of the English climate, but the story goes that he found him an exasperating employer. "I prepare for him a *longue de veau en surprise;* he eats it and doesn't understand what it is!" In disgust, Carême created a last sauce before he left England to express the finality of his decision. Fittingly he called it *La dernière pensée de Carême.* Whether or not this is true, it is a fact that try as George IV would to persuade Carême to return, he refused.

Czar Alexander I was equally unsuccessful when he tried to persuade Carême to come to Russia. In this case Carême's refusal may have been due to resentment because he was forced to help prepare the victory banquet after Napoleon's final defeat. Carême had served Alexander as a temporary chef in Paris, after Napoleon's first defeat by the Allies. But to officiate at the celebration of the second defeat of the emperor he admired, especially after the near-triumph of the Hundred Days, was too much for Carême. In the end he did as he was ordered, being a practical man. But he declined to serve Alexander further.

As it turned out, the victory banquet demonstrated Carême's mettle when faced with the kind of culinary crisis that had destroyed Vatel in the seventeenth century. In this case it was a shortage of gelatin, not fish. An insufficient quantity arrived for Carême's invention, *charlottes Parisienne,* which he planned to feature on the cold buffet in his charge. Nevertheless he ordered the *charlottes* prepared, hoping they would hold up despite the curtailed gelatin. They collapsed. Carême, composed of starch and persistence, did not. Later this cold *entremet* became known as *charlotte Russe.* Possibly its connection with the Russian festivities changed its name.

Another sweet *entremet* with a Russian connection that appeared at this same time is *Nesselrode pudding,* invented by the French chef of the Russian Count Nesselrode. The presence in Paris of many Russian nobles, who preferred the society and climate of France to their own, was probably the reason a number of Russian specialties entered French cuisine at this time. The two *entremets* vanished into the cuisine without any further Russian identification. After all, they were invented by French chefs. But other Russian dishes, particularly soups and potages of Russian origin preserved their Russian identity.

The most notable Russian contribution to the table was *service à la Russe,* introduced to Parisians around this time by the Russian ambassador to France, Count Kurakine. The prevailing mode was *service à la Française,* the centuries-old custom of placing most of the food on the table at one time. Thus a splendid show of hot and cold dishes, roasts, starches, vegetables, and soups greeted the guests as they entered the dining room, gasped in admiration, and took their seats around the table. It was like sitting down to a lavish buffet table. If the meal was very grand the table was replenished midway through the meal with additional dishes.

Service à la Française was meant to dazzle with its beauty and bounty, but too often the food had been waiting for some time before the guests came to the table; hot food had grown cold and tasteless, cold food had lost its refreshing quality. Another disadvantage was the fixed location of the serving dishes. A guest's place at the table often determined what he might dine on. If he was seated near *longe de veau à la Montglas,* but might have preferred *selle de mouton d'Ardennes* at the other end, he could hunger in vain. The huge platter of mutton would usually be passed only to those reasonably near it.

In *service à la Russe* the guests were greeted by a table bare of food but richly ornamented with a centerpiece of flowers flanked by candelabra or epergnes filled with sweetmeats, or both. Roasts were carved at a sideboard and all other food was brought in courses from the kitchen. Everything hot was served piping hot. As Carême expressed it after a visit to St. Petersburg, "The eyes do not devour the first act of dinner as in France . . . but there is the charm of surprise, for every five minutes gourmandise is presented. One does not wait for the amphitryon flaunting his pretentious carving and his anecdotes. [He meant Cambacérès.] A *maître d'hôtel* at a buffet quickly carves the Ukrainian beef, the veal from Archangel, the Volga sturgeon, and the turkey from Périgord. All the plates are presented by a crowd of valets, the service is a marvel, and we eat hot food."

Regardless of these advantages, when *service à la Russe* was first introduced to French society loud objections were raised against any spread of this Russian notion. Let the Russians have their soup hot, the French cried; *they* preferred the profusion of choices that the French way offered, and furthermore, how could one judge what quantity to eat of a dish, not knowing what was to follow—and even more important, how could one adequately measure the bounty of a host?

Service à la Russe did not spread in France, nor elsewhere in Europe, without considerable opposition. Alexander Dumas père, a leading gastronome, grumbled, "You see the platter, but it is positioned far from you, and instead of getting the piece you want, you get what the server brings you."

The English were particularly stubborn. Charles Dickens was roundly criticized in the 1860s for following *service à la Russe* when he entertained. A. V. Kirwan complained, "If you ask nine out of every ten what they mean by dining *à la Russe* they are unable to tell you. All they can say is that there is nothing on the table but flowers and fruits, that the dishes are carved on the sideboard and handed about." He went on indignantly, "I could never see any good reason for its introduction . . . why the English . . . should copy the Russians in the system of dinner-giving—a people who, a century ago, were plunged in the deepest barbarism, and who, as yet, are scarcely half-civilized. Even now the Russians have not in their language any word which conveys the idea of gentleman, and the title of Prince, so common among them, is not much more than a hundred years old."

Carême, too, came around to second thoughts. "This service is perhaps quite agreeable for a small family meal, but for a large gathering it cannot compare with the French method. Our way is by far the most splendid and imposing." Furthermore, he now suspected it was all a money-saving device and tattled about the close watch kept on larder expenditures at the Russian court.

His tongue wagged as well about the pretentious Russian custom of changing plates and cutlery for each course. All well and good, he said, were it not that fastidious diners feared the cutlery was returned unwashed. "This elegance of service exposes you to the danger of eating with the forks of everyone. I have seen women cling to their table settings to avoid this very danger."

It remained for some of Carême's successors, particularly the influential chef Urbain Dubois, to make *service à la Russe* acceptable during the Second Empire and to bring other changes to the French table, such as an end to switching the fork from the left hand to the right (which was the custom in France until the mid-nineteenth century).

Carême continued to be the main influence on the cuisine as France proceeded through two Bourbon monarchies and the rule of the "Citizen King" Louis Philippe. When ruptures developed, as they had a way of doing in France during the nearly half a century that it oscillated between empire, monarchy, and republic, Louis Philippe followed his predecessor Charles X into hasty exile. Louis XVIII had managed to die with dignity in 1824, while on the job, ruling. (Both Louis XVIII and Charles X were the younger brothers of Louis XVI.)

It was now the turn of Napoleon's nephew, Charles Louis Napoleon Bonaparte, known as Louis Napoleon until he declared himself Napoleon III in 1850, and the Second Empire began. During his reign French cuisine enlarged its borders further and took on an international flavor.

Frontispiece of Carême's Le Maître d'hôtel Francais.

The *Grande Cuisine* Becomes Grander

"Dinner was large, luminous, sumptuous."

Thomas Carlyle

I f one word were to describe the Second Empire, flamboyant would serve. It characterized everything about the reign of Napoleon III, including the cuisine, which became increasingly ostentatious as Carême's disciples outdid their master. To some observers it seemed a return to the hedonism of the eighteenth-century Regency under the Duc d'Orléans. The difference now was in the participants—no longer a small inner circle, but all of Paris. Parisians were caught up in an exuberant spirit that verged on frenzy, and Paris, to the world, was the incarnation of the Empire.

The English Captain Rees Howell Gronow, a frequent visitor to France, described the mood. *"Vive le plaisir!* is the cry of the Parisian population . . . they invoke it . . . as far as they can manage it, they strive to make life one joyous holiday." Offenbach set the mood to music in *La Vie Parisienne* with the wild kicking of the cancan, introduced to Parisians not long before from conquered Algeria.

In good part the mood was euphoria, a hopeful response to the political and economic rejuvenation that the new reign seemed to promise. The moment the imperial crown was secure on his head Napoleon III launched a vast reconstruction program for Paris. What was still a medieval city with narrow streets where churches, palaces, petit-bourgeois homes, and slums mingled in aimless confusion was gradually converted into the beautiful city of spacious parks and wide boulevards, the latter possibly designed for an easy sweep by cannon fire in case of future insurrections. The rebuilding, under the direction of Baron Haussmann, took years to complete, creating employment for the working class and a general feeling of accomplishment among all Frenchmen.

A scintillant court also helped to create the feeling of better times. When a pretty Spanish noblewoman, Eugénie de Montijo, caught Napoleon's eye and refused to yield him the privilege of her bed without marriage, the French happily welcomed an Empress and a return to the glamor of former Napoleonic times. Winterhalter painted the fashionable beauties of the court in their resplendent gowns and deepened the *déjà vu* feeling of the Second Empire.

When the Englishman Charles Worth arrived in Paris to establish what became the French couture, Eugénie and her following eagerly responded to these new winds of fashion, to the delight of Napoleon III. A confirmed Anglophile after years of exile in London, where he had become a popular member of English society, he endorsed almost anything English.

Gastronomically he was more English than French. He had even brought along his English chef, Evans, when he returned to France. But the cuisine that flourished around him was not affected by his taste for simple food; instead it duplicated his love of pageantry, which dictated colorful uniforms at every turn. Guards in sky-blue tunics over white breeches, plumed metal helmets and metal breast plates glinting in the sun, stood outside the palace. The royal couriers flashed through the streets in green and gold livery and cockaded hats. Grenadiers bristled with fierce mustaches and fur bus-

Typical pièces montées *that decorated* grande *tables during the Second Empire.*

bys; Algerian Zouaves in red jackets, blue pantaloons, and tasseled fezes added an exotic touch. Paris had the appearance of an operetta in dress rehearsal.

The cuisine of the Second Empire was equally dramatic. Later, when it was put together in a volume for the English public, the London *Spectator* complained that its excessive garnishes and sculptures in fat "suggested the bad days when patricians thought it good taste to send up fawns whole, or when naked dwarfs jumped out of Czar Peter's pies." But it was all part of the march of the *grande cuisine* to a broader and more international level.

Napoleon III contributed to this expansion when he staged two international expositions in Paris—in 1855 and 1867—and invited the world to come and see the restored glory of France. Many nations exhibited their wares and cuisines. Mary K. Waddington, the American wife of a resident Frenchman, reported, "All the world flocked to Paris."

For her the 1855 exposition was more dust and confusion than pleasure. "It was certainly neither pleasant nor comfortable—even in the most expensive restaurants . . . all overcrowded, very bad service, badly lighted, and generally bad food."Chauvinistically she declared the American restaurant at the exposition to be the best. "There I had a very good breakfast one morning, with delicious waffles made by a Negro cook," she said, dealing a crushing blow to the French croissant.

The five million visitors who came to the 1855 exposition filled Paris with a babel of languages that soon echoed in the first important presentation of French cuisine since Carême: *La Cuisine Classique* (1856), perhaps the largest and surely the heaviest culinary gathering up to that time.

The authors, Urbain Dubois and Emile Bernard, were chefs in the Paris homes of the Polish counts Uruski and Krasinski. Dubois, already a leader among his contemporaries, gave as his credentials, "Chef and pastry cook under chef Haas in the House of Rothschild." Bernard cited no previous background and in any case soon receded from the culinary scene, while Dubois continued to grow in prominence and produced a large body of works.

The international cuisine now followed in hotels and restaurants is discernible in the pages of *La Cuisine Classique.*

Portrait of Urbain Dubois from L'Art Culinaire.

Actually, its beginnings were apparent at the end of the First Empire, filtering down from the tables of international diplomats. Carême had described in his *L'Art de la Cuisine Française* such Russian and Polish specialties as borscht, tschy (a cabbage soup), ouka (a fish soup), rosolli (a rice soup), plus a scattering of dishes from other nations, including a few *potages americaines de tortue, à la Washington* and *à la New York. Soupe* was rarely used in the modern sense until much later and potages were usually substantial dishes, like stews.

Carême's "foreigners" were a mere driblet compared to the number in *La Cuisine Classique*. Polish dishes were many, reflecting the nationality of the authors' employers. *Potage Batwina*, a cold soup of sorrel and spinach cooked in *kvas*, a Russian beverage similar to beer, was served with mounds of thinly sliced cucumber, shellfish, braised sturgeon and salmon, all of this sprinkled with grated horseradish root and added to the soup as it was eaten. *Potage Krapiwa*, served hot, presented sausages on a bed of puréed sorrel, spinach, and white nettles. The garnish it wore was strictly French, however, *Œufs farcis frits* (stuffed cooked eggs, fried), presented by Marin in 1739, and probably introduced to Poland by that devotee of fine dining King Stanislaus, whose daughter was queen of France at the time.

Sandwiches made their bow to French cooks in *La Cuisine Classique*. Gnocchi, *noques Allemande* and *gnoquis à la Romaine* appear to be newcomers—at least they are not present in Carême's *L'Art de la Cuisine Française*. Other new dishes may have become known to chefs before they appeared in print, and this may have been true of the French delight *pommes soufflés*, accidentally invented in 1837 by chef-proprietor Collinet of the Pavillon Henry IV in Sainte-Germain-en-laye. When the preparation of *pommes frites* was unexpectedly halted midway and resumed a few minutes later, *zut alors!* a new dish was born. Its appearance in *La Cuisine Classique* seems to be its first.

La Cuisine Classique reached well beyond Carême's *L'Art de la Cuisine Française*—and high time, Dubois asserted in his introduction. "While we affirm our profound deference to the master [Carême], no one in his right mind will insist that his is the last word on our noble profession." In Dubois' opinion a good many words, or, more specifically, dishes, needed to be added. "*La grande cuisine* is long overdue for some bold and modern treatment," he declared. "Since no one has as yet come forward to do this, we have created a well-conceived book, embracing all the branches of the culinary art, illuminated by the traditions of the past but including the modern school in all its splendor."

That splendor was illustrated in numerous large steel engravings of platters occupied by whole fish, massive roasts, coveys of birds, or assemblages of crustaceans, all of them garnished and decorated beyond recognition. Several hundred smaller illustrations were a guide to ostentation on a smaller scale. Dubois' modern treatment more suited to the lavish all-at-once exhibition of *service à la Française* and even more pretentious than in the past, was certainly at odds with his ringing declaration in favor of the simpler *service à la Russe* in the same volume. "Aside from its other advantages, this book asserts our support of that new method of serving that is advancing upon us with rapid strides, *service à la Russe*. By popularizing this method we prepare all of you who are forward-looking and say to you, face the future now; that's all!"

La Cuisine Classique had the field pretty much to itself until 1867, when another prominent chef of the Second Empire, Jules Gouffé, produced a competitor, *Le Livre de Cuisine*. An English writer and gastronome, George Sala, acclaimed it "One of the best French cookery books of modern times." Gouffé had served under Carême as a pastry chef and was esteemed by fellow chefs as a true disciple of that master. The chefs' periodical *L'Art Culinaire*, founded in 1882, reverently bracketed them: "*Gloire à vous, Carême et Gouffé.*"

Le Livre de Cuisine was closer in format and content to Beauvilliers than Carême. It appealed to both professional and home cooks but separated the two cuisines and dealt with each individually. For home cooks the recipes were simpler and gave instructions and quantities. The expected results could indeed be produced by a home cook, who could rely on radish roses or pickle fans (carefully explained) to ornament a dish. But the section dealing with *La Grande Cuisine* was as grand as anything in *La Cuisine Classique;* any dish prepared with less than five garnishes was virtually bare.

Le Livre de Cuisine strove to be as French as the tricolor. "I've omitted nothing except pomposity, charlatanism, the ridiculous, unknown dishes which no one eats and which encumber other books, and the wornout ideas disguised under new names," Gouffé said, dismissing most of the new dishes inducted by his predecessors. He stood firmly for the status quo in gastronomy, including *service à la Francaise.* "Decoration is an important part of *la grande cuisine,*" he asserted. "To cut up portions in advance tends to destroy the fine art of decorating at which most chefs excel. At a single stroke this might tend to destroy the external beauty of our *grande cuisine,* which has made it the star of the first rank among other cuisines."

Meanwhile Dubois, now chef to the king of Prussia, continued to advance his international viewpoint. In the same year, almost as if answering Gouffé, he produced an even more cosmopolitan work: *Cuisine de tous les pays, Etudes Cosmopolités.* This new and dense collection of 1288 recipes included Spanish gazpacho, Arabian cuscus, India's kadjiori (in England it was converted to kedgeree), buckwheat pancakes and Indian corn cakes from America, and German dishes such as duck with sauerkraut, beer soup, stuffed cabbage, and ways of preparing most meats and vegetables "German" style, gleaned from his recent experience in the royal German kitchen.

He added to the numerous Polish and Russian dishes in the first work. One dubious entry was bears' paws, "common as pigs' feet in Russian markets, and prepared in the same way," Dubois explained. "They may appeal to people of the West," he added in the English translation of the work published in 1886. One assumes he meant Americans.

Among the French dishes, *glace au four* appears to be a newcomer which eventually evolved into Baked Alaska. This

The garde manger. *Chaudfroids and other elaborate delicacies were prepared here. "The machine to* haché *(see at left) and the* mortier *for* farces *(on table) are characteristic of this division," said Dubois. Foods were stored in the* garde manger; *meats, poultry, and fish were kept fresh in the ice chest in the center of the room. Live fish probably resided temporarily in the sink.*

The kitchen of a grande *home, as illustrated by Dubois in* La Cuisine Artistique, *was arranged in divisions. This was the central kitchen where small meals and* petit dejeuners *could be prepared by one or two chefs. Note the table with ink stand at right, probably for the* chef de cuisine.

The pastry kitchen, with special ovens suitable for preparing delicate pastries. Molds, utensils, and decorations for pièces montées *(in cupboard) give some idea of the dishes prepared here.*

The rotisserie *division. Roasts,* grillades, *and entrements other than desserts were prepared here.*

baked-meringue-over-ice-cream dessert is said to have been invented in Paris around 1867 by a Chinese chef with the Chinese mission. The mission was probably in Paris for the second exposition. In any case, presenting this novelty was a neat piece of one-upmanship for Dubois.

He continued to expound the virtues of *service à la Russe* in *Cuisine de tous les pays,* and also turned his attention to another reform he hoped to sell to his countrymen: the fork in the left hand.

Clearly, in 1869 the French were accustomed to switching forks from left hand to right after cutting a morsel of food, as most Americans still do. The nonswitch evidently started in class-conscious England, where retaining the fork in the left hand became one of the many shibboleths the upper class devised to set its members apart. Dubois dwelt on the cachet of this relatively new practice, "the method most observed and practiced in the higher circles of [English] society." It was also sensible and convenient. "Soon it will take the lead," he prophesied.

Its exclusivity was soon diluted as the rising middle class of England and the continent adopted it. Even the lower classes, who fed themselves with knives well into the nineteenth cen-

The grande buffet de bal, *produced with regularity in the kitchen quarters of a grande home. From* La Cuisine Artistique *by Urbain Dubois.*

tury, made the transition to the left hand when they began to use forks. Democratic Americans, quick to reject anything that smacked of class-consciousness or affectation, stubbornly clung to the old way.

For urging Frenchmen to eat the English way, and for introducing many dishes prepared "English fashion," the English *Gentleman's Magazine* heaped praise on Dubois: "He was bold enough to teach his continental compeers that England included many noble dishes, and fine table manners, with which they would be wise to make themselves acquainted."

The English press was less favorable to Dubois's *La Cuisine Artistique* (1870). Reviewing the British edition, the *Spectator* called it "a book for German princes, London Lord Mayors, and American millionaires." The English *Saturday Review* compared Dubois unfavorably with Gouffé. In its reviewer's opinion Gouffé met his reader "on a comprehensible level," while Dubois offered "distant visions of Prussian splendor and dinners [fit only] for the monarch or the millionaire." Both Gouffé and Dubois would remain "distant visions" for England's prospering middle class until the late 1880s, when the rising entrepreneur could see what the traveled milord ate by observing him in a public restaurant. Before that time the English aristocracy would as willingly have stalked about naked in the streets as dine in public. A Swiss hotelier and a French *chef de cuisine* changed all that, and made the *grande cuisine* of France known to all Britishers who could afford it.

Restaurants and the *Grande Cuisine*

*"We should look for someone
to eat and drink with
before looking for something
to eat and drink, for dining alone
is leading the life of a
lion or wolf."*

Epicurus

Restaurants brought the *grande cuisine* to the attention of the public much earlier in France than in England. But even there, where the first restaurant was opened in Paris in 1765, the *grande cuisine* came belatedly to the public. As late as 1870 most of its practitioners were employed in private kitchens where its preparation had to please only one employer; in restaurants the *grande cuisine* chef had to please the public.

What became a thriving industry started when an enterprising fellow, Boulanger (he may have been a baker or *boulanger*), began to serve a variety of hot soups as quick energizers—*restaurantes*. When he included a dish of creamed sheep's feet among his soups, protests arose from the *traiteurs*, purveyors of cooked meats, who claimed that only they were permitted to sell such preparations.

Boulanger—or whatever his name was—prevailed and added other such dishes to his menu. He soon had a large and evidently profitable following. Diderot wrote to a friend, "I went to dine at the *restaurateur*'s place in the rue des Poulies; one is treated well there but has to pay dearly for it."

Boulanger's success moved Antoine Beauvilliers, then chef to Louis XVI's brother, the Comte de Provence, to try his hand at the budding industry. In 1782 he opened the Grande Taverne de Londres, in the rue de Richelieu, the first real restaurant in the modern sense. He closed it during the Revolution but bounded back with a larger establishment when it ended. By 1800 more restaurants had appeared, but they catered only to men and demimondaines. Ladies, if ladies they were—actresses, singers and dancers were of questionable reputation—did not visit public cafés and restaurants until the First Empire was well established, and then only in the evening, usually after the theater. During the day restaurants and cafés continued to be the province of males. To Frenchmen they were like the private clubs of Englishmen. There were English coffee houses as well in Paris, but Lord Chesterfield warned his son not to visit them. "[They] are by no means creditable at Paris . . . the resort of the scrub English . . . and attainted Scotch and Irish." In both countries the literati had frequented coffee houses (cafés to the French) long before Boulanger began to serve his *restaurantes*.

The Mille Colonnes cafe in Paris. Captain Gronow reported that it was popular with English visitors in the early 19th century.

Cafés were the headquarters of the leading young hotheads and intellectuals of the Revolution. By all accounts the "most illustrious and popular" was the Café de Foy, whose proprietor, M. Joussereau, merits fond remembrance for giving Paris restaurants the first of their picturesque outdoor dining spots. Gilded chairs in the garden permitted Joussereau's patrons to enjoy his delicious sherbets under the chestnut trees.

Under these same chestnut trees of the Café de Foy, Camille Desmoulins, one of the prominent Revolutionaries who frequented it, launched the idea of the Revolutionary cockade. He plucked a leaf from a tree and stuck it in his hat, intending only to amuse the crowd, but it instantly became a symbol.

The Goncourt brothers, the French litterateurs and social historians of the nineteenth century, speculated that the forerunner of midday luncheon was conceived at the time of the Revolution at another popular café, the Café Hardy, which later developed into a full-scale restaurant.

Madame Hardy astutely recognized that the sessions of the Revolutionary Convention, which began at noon and lasted until six in the evening, were too long to be sustained by the meager morning *petit déjeuner*. She persuaded her husband to introduce an informal buffet service of sturdier foods — kidneys, sausages, grilled chops, and the like — for those who came to the café to have coffee and a biscuit before the sessions began.

Because these sturdier foods required a fork, the term *déjeuner à la fourchette* was applied, and the meal quickly became a national custom. By 1816 Lady Morgan reported, "The *déjeuner à la fourchette*, taken in the middle of the day, is among the most fashionable entertainments of Paris during the spring season." Eventually it became *déjeuner*, the midday meal. England followed with lunch.

First-class restaurants were still few in 1810, when Grimod de la Reynière observed, "There are numerous restaurants in Paris at present, but few really good ones. Those who have the crowd today may be empty tomorrow if their cuisine ceases to be good." At the top of the list he placed Les Frères Provencaux, the Véry, and the Rocher de Cancale, which he

Illustration from L'Art Culinaire.

called "the peak of Tenerife in the world of gastronomy." Previously he had accorded Beauvilliers' restaurant a peak.

The Rocher de Cancale catered to such noted gastronomes as Brillat-Savarin and Balzac. Baron Pückler-Muskau, also a gastronome of note, if the number of dishes named for him at the time is an indication, had admired the Rocher in its earlier days, but thought otherwise when he visited Paris in the 1830s. "Some of the most eminent restaurants I have visited have somewhat degenerated," he complained, "particularly the once celebrated Rocher de Cancale."

To slight the Rocher verged on blasphemy to French gastronomes, though later another dissident, a Frenchman at that, questioned the originality of one of the Rocher's most vaunted dishes: *sole Normande.* Chef Langlais of the Rocher claimed its invention. Not so, said the dissident; Langlais had merely adapted Carême's *ragoût de matelot Normande* and added egg yolk to the fish-based cream sauce. The question is, why call it Normande in the first place, since the most distinctive Normandy addition would be a hint of apples, or at least apple brandy or cider in the preparation of a dish?

The Rocher's *chef d'œuvre* still endures in name, but its modern preparation differs somewhat from the Carême and Langlais versions.

French restaurants continued to cater chiefly to men until the Second Empire, when entire families of the bourgeoisie began to dine out during the Paris Exposition. Captain Gronow on another visit from England in the 1860s described Paris as "a city of cafés and restaurants . . . foreigners arriving in Paris seem by instinct to rush to them." As for the French, they practically took up residence. "Paris is proverbially fond of dining out; in fact, the social intercourse may be said to take place more frequently in the public café than under the domestic roof."

The Goncourts were especially disturbed by this devotion to restaurants. Edmond Goncourt recorded his dismay: "My Paris, the Paris of the manners of 1830 to 1848, is vanishing, both materially and morally. Social life is in the way of a great evolution. I see [whole families with their children] in the cafes. The home is dying. Life threatens to become public . . . making one think of some American Babylon of the future." He concluded, "It is stupid to live in a time of growth."

By then the Rocher and Beauvilliers' restaurant had closed and been replaced by newer *luxe* names, the Véfour, Bignon's, Laurent, Moulin Rouge; but in a city now crowded with restaurants perhaps eight in all could correctly be termed first class, with a kitchen ruled by a master chef practicing the *grande cuisine*.

In ordinary restaurants, service was *table d'hôte* (table of the host). The diner could order only what the restaurant had prepared, or chose to prepare from a fixed menu. For that matter, even at a Rothschild table the diner was obliged to eat what the host served. It was different in the *grande cuisine* restaurants, where diners chose from a list of suggestions or *carte* (*service à la carte*) or could gratify a special yearning by ordering a dish not on the *carte*.

Diners could enjoy complete privacy if they chose, in a *cabinet particulier*. In these private quarters the fate of a nation might be planned by a few statesmen, but more often the *cabines* were devoted to affairs of a more romantic nature, as their furnishings made plain. The limited but luxurious appointments usually included an inviting couch for an amorous prelude or postlude to a meal. In some restaurants a couple could enter the *cabines* through a private outside entrance.

The Moulin Rouge, one of the newest of the *grande cuisine* restaurants, discreetly screened its private entrance with lilac bushes. Thanks to this landscaping the restaurant became wildly popular with *cabine* frequenters. Its admirable cuisine was soon renowned as well for its extravagant cost; one dinner for four came to 2400 francs, the equivalent of five hundred dollars at the time.

The London journalist Felix Whitehurst, who kept London informed about Parisian activities during the summer season, reported: "I know of no more characteristic scene than that nightly to be viewed at this season at the Moulin Rouge, where Bardoux [the proprietor] 'restores' a grateful public. The garden is closely packed with tables; around it are arbors for ladies and gentlemen dining tête-à-tête . . . music arises . . . looking up you are aware [of couples] mingling dancing with dining in the *cabinets* . . . there is a glorious moon actually dimming the gas, and as the diner inhales the fresh air he blesses Bardoux and feels thankful."

Had Whitehurst penetrated to the kitchen he would have found it in sharp contrast to the scene he described. In the boiler-room atmosphere perspiring cooks and scullions raced about wildly. Shouts and curses filled the air, most of them issuing from the throat of Ulysse Rohan, the remarkable chef responsible for the cuisine that brought crowds to the Moulin Rouge. Rohan was acknowledged to be a master at dealing with the multiple demands of *service à la carte*, a task more challenging than managing the kitchen of a prince.

Like most of his contemporaries, Rohan believed it impossible to govern a kitchen *"sans une pluie de gifles,"* a shower of slaps. These were often delivered with little provocation, and usually to the newest or youngest member of the kitchen staff. In 1865 this dubious distinction fell to a young *commis* recently arrived from Nice. His name was Escoffier.

A Little Chef
from Nice

*"A good cook is the peculiar gift of
the gods. He must be a perfect
creature from the brain to the
palate, from the palate to the finger's end."*

Walter Savage Landor

In the modest restaurant Chez Philippe in Nice,
M. Bardoux, proprietor of the elegant Moulin
Rouge in Paris, ordered *Langouste Niçoise*, the restaurant's
new specialty. A friend had called it to Bardoux's attention
when he arrived in Nice to scout for recruits for his kitchen
staff, a common practice among Paris restaurateurs. Nice
seemed to produce culinary talent as abundantly as it grew
flowers.

Three bites of the lobster, and Bardoux searched out the
young chef who had devised the dish. He was new to Chez
Philippe, but had served several years of apprenticeship in
Nice, including a few years in the restaurant of his uncle,
Jean Escoffier. Bardoux persuaded the nineteen-year-old chef
to come to the Moulin Rouge as *commis-rôtisseur*. There he
would be in charge of roasts and cooked meats, and he would
prepare his *Langouste Niçoise*. Now it would be an exclusive
specialty at the Moulin Rouge.

Not for long, it seems. The dish was soon copied by another restaurant and renamed *Lobster Armoricaine*. Later it became *Lobster Americaine*. Like *Sole à la Normande*, it set off an endless debate about its origin.

There was no question about who originated it, said Phileas Gilbert, himself a noted chef, writer, and later Escoffier's collaborator on *Le Guide Culinaire*. Gilbert claimed that Escoffier often referred to it as "My first chef d'œuvre."

By 1867 Escoffier had advanced to *garde-manger*, in charge of the cold buffet. The second Paris Exposition opened to the same spendthrift mood that had characterized the exposition of 1855. The same attention focused on the culinary arts and drew crowds to the established dining temples. New ones were encouraged to open. When the exposition ended, restaurants continued to prosper, attracting Parisians for whom dining out had become another form of entertainment, as the Goncourts had noted. Less expensive restaurants fed entire families. Duval's, one of the earliest and least expensive, opened branches and became the forerunner of modern fast-food chains. The wealthy bourgeoisie and visitors to Paris, especially those from England, patronized the *grande cuisine* restaurants.

There was little concern over rumblings of political unrest; after all, this had been constant since the Revolution. The Second Empire appeared to be secure. Few could see that its underpinnings were hollow and ready to crumble. Saber rattling in Prussia, weakening ties with Italy and England, even rumors of the Emperor's ill-health, failed to distract Parisians from their main concern which was pleasure, undiluted.

As the summer of 1870 began, the usual crowd of bon vivants filled the garden of the Moulin Rouge nightly. The kitchen echoed with shouted orders. Bardoux beamed. Rohan energetically cuffed the ears of scullions. When the *chef saucier* defected to a rival restaurant Rohan appointed Escoffier to the post—the last step before attaining *chef de cuisine*. Escoffier wondered *when* he would take that last step—and *where*, since Rohan seemed firmly settled at the Moulin Rouge for years ahead. The answer came with unexpected swiftness in July 1870.

Pen and ink sketch by Charles Bertall, 19th century.

Napoleon III, maneuvered by Bismarck into an ill-advised confrontation, declared war on Prussia. The next day the French minister of war demanded a dozen cooks of the Societé des Cuisiniers des Paris for divisions of the Grand Army of the Rhine. Events happened so quickly "that the echo of the summons had hardly receded," Escoffier wrote in his army memoirs (*Memoirs d'un Soldat de l'Armée du Rhin*), when he and a fellow cook at the Moulin Rouge were called from its kitchen and dispatched to the Rhine Army headquarters.

Escoffier was made *chef de cuisine* to a Colonel d'Andlau, who may rightly have nursed dreams of feasting like a Talleyrand with a chef from the famed Moulin Rouge at his command. Such anticipation was short-lived. The French forces were swiftly defeated and withdrew to Metz, where they remained under siege, unable to obtain food from outside. Luckily Escoffier had rounded up some chickens, a pig, a sheep, and a goat, which were put under guard. The goat was his "chief treasure," supplying milk daily for Béchamel sauce and other niceties. "Like all others, I was forced to economize and plan carefully," Escoffier wrote. "But I never failed to give my officers an abundant table: at each meal a soup, an entrée or roast, a salad, an *entremet* of fruit, and finally coffee and cognac. By comparison with what other officers had, it was positively sardanapalesque."

Culinary legerdemain became a daily exercise. Turnips masqueraded as potatoes, prepared as if they were: served in fluffy mounds, gratinéed or sautéed to golden crispness, and often garnished with truffles. By some quirk of the fortunes of war, truffles were easier had than potatoes. When only horsemeat remained to him, Escoffier disguised it in stews and even made it into a meat salad with eggs and mayonnaise.

Parisians were obliged to be equally ingenious, resorting to more exotic flesh during the siege of Paris. The entire zoo was conscripted to fill Parisian stomachs, monied stomachs for the most part. Felix Whitehurst reported to his English readers, "The fact is, there are sufficient *'viandes de luxe'* for the rich, such as monkey, jackal, bear, deer, young gazelle, antelope, elephant and lion."

Less fortunate Parisians who could not afford to patronize restaurants, or to pay the price that exotic zoo flesh commanded in markets, daily foraged for cats, rats, and mice to bring meat to their tables. A Daumier drawing for *Chari-Vari* shows a queue of Parisians crouching in a gutter, waiting their turn to capture a rat as the creatures emerged from a sewer hole.

More serious than food shortages were the political crises that loomed as the war ended, and with it the Second Empire.

Daumier drawing of Parisians waiting for rats to emerge from a sewer. The rodents came to many Parisian tables during the Prussian siege of Paris.

Escoffier returned to Paris in March 1871 to find "Traces of the war everywhere—a mad world . . . I sensed that the people of Paris wanted to resume their accustomed life—but what a vain hope!" He was witness to the seventy-one day insurrection against the Commune but refused to participate. "On the 18th of March the cannons in Montmartre, taken there by the National Guard, bombarded the city. April 6th big placards were posted by the Comité Central calling all men between eighteen and forty to arms for the defense of the Commune. I did not wish to become a soldier of the insurrection; on the contrary, my military status obliged me to rejoin the regular army. Knowing that all departures from the city would be prevented within hours, I did not wait a minute but ran to the Gare St. Lazare. Luckily I was able to board the very last train that left Paris freely."

After another eighteen months in the army as a chef Escoffier returned to civilian life and went at once to the South of France to visit his family. Astonishing changes had occurred in the seven years since he left. Nice and the surrounding area reaching to Monaco were now fashionable. Those who counted themselves members of society felt obliged to appear there sometime during the long "season," December to April; those who aspired to society went in hope of eventual acceptance.

Almost a century earlier the Niçois district had received its first boost from Tobias Smollett in his *Travels in France and Italy* (1766), with praise for Nice's months of "charming blue expanse [of sky] with never a speck of cloud." But the grand influx had begun in the early 1860s, traceable in large part to several coincidental events.

The spread of railroads, which Napoleon III had encouraged, made it fairly easy to reach the curving Riviera with its balmy climate lasting nearly all year long. Formerly the only means had been the post-chaise and the larger diligence.

A plebiscite in 1860 took Nice from Sardinia and restored it to France, encouraging hotelkeepers seeking new sites to look kindly at the area as a place to build.

Queen Victoria bestowed cachet by taking a villa in nearby Menton, bringing English artistocrats and her royal relatives in her wake. (The lovely Boulevard des Anglais in the city of Nice testifies to this early British interest in the area.)

And last, or perhaps first, an edict against gambling, issued in Prussia in 1858 and affecting most of its popular spas, brought François Blanc, operator of the gambling casino at Bad Homburg, to Monaco. There he took over the struggling gambling concession that Prince Charles of Monaco had permitted to open in the hope of raising revenue for his tiny realm.

Where gambling went, British and European nobility and monied travelers from everywhere followed, equating the healthful properties of climate and waters with the lure of gaming tables. If anything they preferred the latter. Without gambling a resort was dead when it most needed to be alive, in the evening when boredon was likely to set in.

At Bad Homburg, Blanc had dreamed of making that spa the dominant resort of Europe, and himself a latter-day Beau Nash. Instead he made the casino at Monte Carlo the ultimate symbol of gambling, and himself a legendary figure. A popular ditty soon went the length of the expanding Riviera. "Whether one plays the black or the red, it is always white (*blanc*) who wins." (A noted exception was Charles Deville Ward, who "broke the bank at Monte Carlo" in 1891. The casino could stand any size win by then.) In 1863 Blanc formed the Societé des Bains des Mer et Cercle des Etrangers (Sea Bathing Society and Foreigners' Club) which became the corporate name of the casino and its holdings and soon sheltered an exceedingly lucrative enterprise.

The roulette wheels spun briskly in Monte Carlo when Escoffier returned from his army service in 1871. He saw that the future of the sunny coast was promising. Still, for a chef of twenty-seven who hoped to reach the top of his profession, Paris held the most promise. But that would mean returning to the Moulin Rouge as a subordinate after heading his own kitchen in the army. While Escoffier debated his next move, the new Hotel Luxembourg in Nice offered him the post of

A diligence, the favored means of transportation before rail-roads became available.

chef de cuisine. He accepted. Six months later Rohan left the Moulin Rouge to open his own restaurant and Bardoux offered Escoffier the post.

Once back in Paris, Escoffier began some of the reforms he longed to introduce into restaurant kitchens. He had experimented with a few in the army, and since prudence dictated a cautious start he began as he had there, by reducing the noise. Orders would no longer be shouted by the aptly named *l'aboyeur* (barker), he told the staff. He renamed that individual *l'annonceur,* and cautioned the others to keep their voices correspondingly low. "The rush hour is not the signal for a rush of words," he told them. The staff laughed and willingly accepted the innovations. It was a small beginning but it would grow, and Escoffier's reputation along with it as he introduced other reforms.

Paris Is Herself Again

*"Strange to see how a good
dinner and feasting reconciles
everybody."*
Samuel Pepys

N ever long to convalesce after any convul-
sion, the French displayed even greater
recuperative powers after the fall of the Second Empire. Despite a change of presidents twice in two years and a continuing struggle between Republicans and Monarchists, the
strength of the Third Republic (which would endure for
seventy-two years) was evident at its outset.

Paris was again the gayest capital in the world. Parisians
returned to peacetime pleasures as if there had been no interruption. New works by Bizet and Wagner were the rage; Offenbach was still a favorite. Performances took place before
audiences that rivaled the stage for brilliance. Jewels and extravagant Worth gowns brought gasps from onlookers who
packed the opera house to the gallery's last row. When fire
destroyed the opera house a new one was built that is still
one of the beauties of Paris.

Every possible occasion was used for a celebration. France

Pen and ink sketch by Charles Bertall, 19th century.

had abolished its own monarchy, but monarchs from other countries were welcomed with lavish ceremony, especially if they ruled an exotic or far-off land. The state visit of the shah of Persia was acknowledged with impressive military reviews, fireworks, and gala spectacles attended by Parisians of all ages and classes.

The carefree mood seemed unchanged from the days of Napoleon III. George Sala, in Paris at the time, described it: "Thousands of well-dressed people . . . sit all day and during a portion of the night, in and outside the boulevard cafés, smoking, drinking, playing at cards and dominoes, and otherwise enjoying themselves . . . they are imbibing coffee and cognac at 8:00 after dinner, they are consuming ices and sorbets at 10:00; they are sipping American grog at midnight . . . [whole] families, grandams of eighty who drink hot rum-punch, little brats of seven who drink hocks."

Sala's Parisians were not to be found at the Moulin Rouge. Instead, as Escoffier wrote in his reminiscences of its celebrated clientele, "Princes, dukes, kings of finance and leading political figures gathered."

One of the leading political figures was Leon Gambetta, who had made a spectacular escape by balloon from besieged Paris, helped to end the reign of Napoleon III, then returned to Paris to see the Third Republic through its stormy beginnings. Gambetta dined often at the restaurant, usually in a *cabinet particulier* where, in the proven way of such predecessors as Barras, Talleyrand and Cambacérès, he accomplished political ends over seductive meals.

One such dinner recorded by Escoffier was an early and unofficial attempt by the Prince of Wales to bring about the Entente between France and England. Wales finally succeeded when he became Edward VII. The dinner was served to Gambetta, Charles Dilke of the British Foreign Office, and Wales:

Velouté de poulet au curry
(Curried cream of chicken soup)
Laitances de carpes aux queues d'écrevisses
(Carp roes and crayfish)
Petit Bouchées garnies de purée de champignons
(Puff pastry patties filled with mushroom purée)
Selle d'agneau de Béhague
(Saddle of lamb with sauce of tomatoes and garlic)
Petits pois Anglaises
(Peas tossed in butter)
Suprême de caneton de Rouen en gelée
(Jellied breasts of Rouen duckling)
Blanc de romaine aux œufs
(Hearts of romaine lettuce garnished with riced, boiled egg)
Asperges d'Argenteuil
(Asparagus from Argenteuil region)
Soufflé fromage Périgourdine
(Cheese soufflé garnished with truffles)
Pêches framboise
(Chilled, poached peaches topped with whole or puréed raspberries)
Fleurette chantilly
("Flowers" of whipped cream to garnish peaches)
Macarons de Nancy
(Almond macaroons)

Selle d'agneau de Béhague is especially worth noting because it appeared regularly on menus prepared by Escoffier at the Moulin Rouge and may have been an early example of a trademark or similar commercial identification attesting to the meat's superior quality.

The Count Amadée de Béhague was an authority on agronomy and cattle breeding, two fields of expertise which, combined with substantial land holdings, made him immensely wealthy. He was typical of the new wealth with acquired titles. Béhague's aggressive wife gained entrée for them to exclusive social circles. Soon the Béhagues' extravagant entertainments made their climb swifter and their salons sought after. As Madame de Sévigné had observed two centuries earlier, "Nothing is wanted but money to accomplish everything." The historian Vizetelly later remarked, "You had to wait for your entrée to Béhague *salons* as you might for your election to certain clubs," and gave as an example the experience of a guest who had sought to bring along a friend. "Not this year, my list is full," replied the countess.

At the Moulin Rouge Escoffier often served the lamb with a *provençale* sauce of tomatoes, oil, and garlic. This once caused a young countess to have a tantrum in the *cabinet* where she was dining with her married lover. The lamb, a favorite dish of the couple, had been ordered as usual. This time the countess wanted the recipe for the sauce. Escoffier was summoned to the *cabinet*.

"You need a few cloves of garlic," he began.

"Garlic!" shrieked the countess. "You've been feeding me garlic? What a horror!"

"But, Madame," protested the surprised Escoffier. "You liked the sauce."

"But I detest garlic!" she cried. "How can a restaurant of the *première classe* serve garlic to its patrons? How can you make me reek of the stuff?"

"But, Madame, you didn't reek of it; you couldn't even taste it," said Escoffier, and went on to describe the virtues of garlic, apparently with success. "The cause of garlic was soon won," he noted happily.

Sarah Bernhardt also professed to hate garlic and Escoffier never told her that he added a dash of it to the scrambled eggs he often prepared for her after a performance.

Pen and ink sketch by Charles Bertall.

Garlic aside, once the friendship between Escoffier and the actress began in 1874, it continued to the end of Bernhardt's life. The painter Gustave Doré arranged their first meeting in his studio near the Moulin Rouge. The convenient location brought him often to the restaurant, but occasionally he would order *soupers à deux* to be served in his studio, where he shared them with Bernhardt. "Come meet her," he said one day to Escoffier as he ordered a meal for that evening.

Escoffier recorded the meeting in the flat style that unfortunately mars all his observations about the colorful personalities met during his long career. He was interested only in what they ate.

"Bernhardt adored food," he wrote. "I honestly believe our friendship began when I prepared a timbale of sweetbreads for her that I thickened with a purée of foie gras touched with a hint of cheese and garnished generously with truffles. She absolutely worshipped this savoury dish." The "hint of cheese" was probably grated Gruyère, which Escoffier often added to an otherwise bland or familiar dish to give it a subtle nuance. (A hint of grated Parmesan will do the same for veal or beef fricadelles.)

When Escoffier wrote of food his style quickened, the words gave off an aroma. People, alas, wilted under his pen.

He had none of the venom that splashed Carême's memoirs like ink squirting from a squid. Carême was a prima donna and a gossip. Escoffier was frustratingly discreet—or perhaps merely indifferent. When he did offer anecdotes about the celebrities he knew, they were accounts of such innocent goings-on as the Prince of Wales performing with Bernhardt, if playing a corpse may be called a performance.

In a Sardou play Bernhardt's closing scene took place at the bedside of a murdered prince. Wales, a confirmed Francophile, came often to Paris and regularly attended Bernhardt's performances. One night, for a prank, he occupied the bed as the murdered prince. At once every bon vivant in Paris sought to play the "role."

Whatever Wales did was promptly imitated. Once, suffering from rheumatism in his right shoulder, he kept his elbow close to his body as he shook hands. Imitators were plentiful, untroubled by rheumatism and unaware of the Prince's temporary infirmity.

Giddy Parisian society imitated *its* leaders, who constantly

A waitress in a Duval restaurant. These restaurants were noted for their popular prices and were an early restaurant chain—perhaps the first.

sought to surpass each other. Any pretext would do to stage an entertainment that would set tongues clacking, and, as always, the dinner table was an ideal place to demonstrate superior ingenuity. Prince Galitzin, with Escoffier's help, caused a stir among his friends when he gave a dinner at the Moulin Rouge for Blanche d'Antigny, a sometime actress and full-time courtesan. Galitzin ordered a private dining room to be transformed into a bower of roses. Escoffier carried out the theme with a "rosy" dinner.

A mousseline of smelts was garnished with tiny pink shrimps; the saddle of lamb *de Béhague* was appropriately *à point*, its pinkness enhanced by the red tomato sauce; the *coupe d'Antigny*, a confection of strawberry sherbet that concluded the meal, was swathed in a pinkish cloud of spun sugar. Years later the Prince recalled it as a memorable moment in "the joyous life" in the early days of the Third Republic.

The Third Republic displayed its accomplishments to the world in the Paris Exhibition of 1878. "It confirmed France's wonderful recovery from its disasters," wrote Vizetelly. Crowds of foreigners and provincials again filled Paris as they had for the previous exhibitions. Spectacular balls quickened the social pace. The *Bal des Artistes*, attended by "celebrities from the stage, the demimonde, the nobility and financial world," showed the heterogeneous mix that now, more than ever, made up the Paris social world. "The brilliance and gaiety of the scene were quite as great as in Imperial days. So far as amusement was concerned, Paris had indeed become herself again. The masses seemed quite as merry as the richer folk."

More Parisians than ever now dined out. The "richer folk" had the Café Riche, the Grande Véfour (which had absorbed the Café Véry), the Moulin Rouge, Chez Bignon, the Restaurant Durand, and the Restaurant Maire. For the masses more *table d'hôte* restaurants had opened, offering large meals at low prices. Duval's, leading feeder of the mass public, obliged by opening additional branches where meals cost a fraction of what was charged elsewhere.

Catering establishments also profited by the public's appetite for entertainment. Party-goers inevitably had to take a turn at party-giving if they wished to continue going; many found that a catering establishment was the easiest answer to reciprocity. Maison Chevet, a leader in the catering field, profited more than most such establishments by reason of its superior services, and the many alternatives it offered: private dining rooms of many sizes, some small enough to accommodate six and one of restaurant size; a ballroom; and the usual catering services supplied to private homes. Maison Chevet was a tasteful, elegant version of similar establishments specializing in catered functions today.

In 1879 M. Chevet persuaded Escoffier to become director of the business. Escoffier had married the previous year and had left the Moulin Rouge when the death of his new father-in-law obliged him to leave Paris to look after the family interests. Because his wife, Delphine, preferred to live in the South of France, Escoffier opened a small seasonal restaurant in Cannes, Le Faison d'Or. He soon decided to sell the restaurant, perhaps because he had no wish to be in his own business, or found it too small to fully engage his interest. The offer from M. Chevet came at this precise moment and Escoffier accepted. He remained with the Maison Chevet for five years, rarely doing any actual work in the kitchen. Apparently he missed it. In 1882 he resumed the active duties of a chef at the Restaurant Maire, the Moulin Rouge having recently closed its doors.

His return to a restaurant kitchen was welcomed with joy by followers from the shuttered Moulin Rouge who now came to the Restaurant Maire when word spread that Escoffier was back. Equally pleased were those of his fellow chefs in restaurants who had ideas about organizing their ranks along modern lines. Many agreed with Escoffier that the Carême school had become outmoded, and that it was time to introduce reforms in restaurant management and cooking. The chefs also spoke of finding a formula that would protect their original creations, or, if not protect, at least give credit where credit was due.

Escoffier was enthusiastic about such plans, as was his friend Phileas Gilbert. The two young chefs in their middle thirties were joined by two elders of their profession, Thomas Genin and Alexandre Tavernet. "We should unite for our future protection," said Genin, hinting darkly at forces that might soon be beyond control. In 1882 they took steps.

The
Age of
Escoffier

Fraternal Chefs

"Chefs who write well are as
necessary as other
littérateurs. We must
understand the theory of
the most ancient arts."

Charles Gerard

French chefs had guarded their kitchen secrets for centuries, even from their own brothers, so it was perhaps with some reluctance that they formed the Societé Culinaire Française in 1882, "to help our colleagues throughout the world by sharing our experiences and inventions with them." It may have been an act of self-preservation.

Though French cuisine continued to be the acknowledged leader of Western cuisines, it had become increasingly international, advancing the status of chefs from other nations. In the face of this growing competition, it was urgent to keep French chefs in demand above all others.

Honorary membership in the Societé was extended to restaurateurs, writers on gastronomy, and noted hosts. Rothschild barons were automatically eligible. The Societé launched an official publication, *L'Art Culinaire*, and declared itself "a banner under which French chefs can unite wherever

they are in the world." They *were* all over the world, through-out Europe, in Asia, South America, and by the hundreds in the United States, where new fortunes and driving social ambitions swelled the demand for chefs.

A serious threat to French chefs loomed at home, growing in French kitchens like a stubborn mold. Female cooks! Little could be gained by calling attention to the threat of foreign chefs, but there was no point in maintaining silence about the females. Phileas Gilbert dealt with them in a series of stinging attacks in *L'Art Culinaire*. He began by calling attention to "articles in some of our press, usually signed by a 'cordon bleu.' Cordon bleu!" he snorted. "These recipes are usually incomprehensible and contrary to all culinary principles."

What rankled most was that women had the audacity to set themselves up as professionals without adequate preparation or experience. "Who among *us* would dare to declare himself qualified with less than ten years of experience?" Gilbert de-manded. He was especially alarmed by the announced inten-tion of the city of Rouen to open a cooking school for women, patterned after a London school where professional status was certified after only two years of training. Worse still, instruction in the French school was to be free.

Women cooks had long enjoyed professional status in England, where they had charge of most upper-class kitchens. In the past they had gone through lengthy apprenticeships, like their male counterparts, but this was no longer deemed necessary.

Alfred Suzanne, chef to the Duke of Bedford and head of the Societé's London chapter, implied that recent so-called professionals were little better than housewives. As for *them*—"The average housewife in this country of workingmen has only the most elementary knowledge of cooking. She knows how to boil potatoes and how to roast or boil a piece of meat. That's all. The casserole and the *poêle* are absolutely unknown to her. She doesn't know what to do with a rabbit. Why, one woman, given a rabbit her husband had shot, tried to pluck it like a chicken!"

Phileas Gilbert knew this could never be said of French housewives. Their cooking was delicious. Most chefs preferred their wives' cooking to their own. (They still do.) He was also mindful that Frenchwomen had usurped a culinary prerogative formerly reserved for men in France, though long in the hands of women in England—writing cookbooks. Anything that smacked of the English way aroused his fear. "We do not want what they have in London, a professional school for women cooks," he thundered. "Some day they will take the place of men!"

The Paris newspaper *Figaro* joined in, possibly urged on by the chefs. If women wanted equal status with men, they must endure training like men, said *Figaro*.

The rhetoric increased as others spoke up. In a final two-page outburst, Gilbert, intransigent to the last, declared, "The simple cuisine of the home is all that is permissible and possible for a woman. The noble work of the chef is forbidden to her, and she has, besides, other duties to perform." His final tirade concluded with a couplet that surely enraged the feminine *poêle* wielders of France:

Laissez les roses aux rosiers
Et la cuisine aux cuisiniers.*

Despite male opposition, some Frenchwomen became famous cooks at the time. Mère Fillioux, a star in the 1880's, still blazed brightly in memory in 1925 when the noted gastronome Curnonsky declared her to have been "one of the greatest *cordon bleus* in the world [and] a good and brave Frenchwoman to boot." He placed her in the mixed company of such twentieth-century stars as Marshal Foch, Anatole France, Kipling, and Mistinguette, the music-hall performer.

In the late nineteenth century Mère Fillioux's *bistrot* in Lyon drew gastronomes from all over France, though she offered an extremely limited menu, "Four or five *plats* that I know well how to make, and I never make any others." *Potage velouté aux truffles, Quenelles au gratin au beurre d'écrivesses, Culs d'artichauts au foie gras,* and *Volaille demideuil.* This last dish, which translates into "chicken in half-mourning," was her most famous specialty, a whole young chicken with slices of truffles inserted between the skin and the flesh of the breast, then poached in a rich chicken stock and served with a *sauce suprême.* By her estimate she had decapitated a half-million chickens for it with her trusty little knife. (The blade is now enshrined in a glass case in the Musée Escoffier in Villeneuve-Loubet.)

When the issue of female cooks quieted down, *L'Art Culinaire* began a crusade to change the names of two basic French sauces, *Allemande* and *Espagnole.* "These sauces are eminently French," said Alexandre Tavenet, leader of the movement to rename them. "Their present names grate and outrage our senses. Carême rose against this stupidity . . . Jules Gouffé denounced this absurdity. Our publication should see that justice is done. This humiliation to our culinary science should end."

French hatred for anything German had mounted since the Franco-Prussian War. *Allemande* sauce had to be renamed, Tavenet insisted, suggesting *sauce à la Parisienne* instead. He

*Leave roses to rose trees, and cooking to chefs.

promised to deal with *Sauce Espagnole* in a later issue, but meanwhile Escoffier pronounced it an unnecessary sauce. This perhaps dimmed its foreseeable future and ended further discussion. The patriotic stand against *Allemande* also came to naught—in the sauce pot. However, serving the Allemande king of Prussia caused Emile Bernard, coauthor with Urbain Dubois of *La Cuisine Classique*, to be hounded out of the chefs' Societé. Dubois, guilty of the same offence, somehow rode out the storm.

As promised, *L'Art Culinaire* was a forum for sharing information, opinions, and anything else that came into its correspondents' heads. A warning was sounded against *"fraudeurs* who are mixing talc into flour and sugar to increase their volume." Action was demanded against the high tax on sugar. "We cannot compete with America's cheap sugar. Our candy trade will suffer," cried the confectioners.

Expensive decorations on restaurant tables drew complaints from restaurateurs intent on keeping down expenses. "The recently introduced custom of using surtouts, flowers, and *pièces* so tall that those to the right cannot see their friend to the left" were labeled "the ostentatious manner of bourgeois *maisons*" by the complainants.

Arguments erupted over trifling points of history: how and when *chaudfroid* received its name. "In 1774 from a chef named Chaufroix in Louis XV's kitchen," said one correspondent. Another disagreed, fixed the date as 1759, the invention an accident in the kitchen of the Marechal de Luxembourg, and denied there was ever a chef named Chaufroix.

Some contributors were longwinded. Alfred Suzanne went on for paragraphs about the English mania for toast. "In France the first question we put to a kitchen applicant is, 'Can you make a *pot-au-feu?* Can you make an omelette?' In England they ask 'Can you make proper toast? For breakfast? For tea? For savories?'" In the end, he concluded that *toast*, like *sandwich*, should be adopted into French. It was an improvement over *la rôtie de pain*.

Many contributors wrote in a grandiose style reminiscent of the Italian chef who amused Montaigne in Catherine de Medici's time. It seems that any chef who could spell fancied

"What name shall I give my soup?" ponders a chef. From
L'Illustration, 1887.

himself a writer. Fortunately, most contributors were content
to stop at recipes.

Every issue carried inspirations from other countries, sent
in by French chefs working there. *Bûche de Noël,* inspired by
the Swiss *bûche* or rolled sponge cake, appeared in an early
issue. *Truites à l'aïoli* (trout in garlic sauce) and Roman
Braciola (rolled flank steak) arrived from Italy. *Bœuf à la
Strogonoff* [sic] was sent by a chef in St. Petersburg. Austrian
sauces laced with horseradish came from Vienna. All were
new at the time to readers of *L'Art Culinaire.* French recipes
were by far the most numerous. Escoffier faithfully contributed recipes throughout the fifteen years *L'Art Culinaire* was
published, and wielded considerable influence from the start.
His numerous menus listed enough dishes to stimulate any
chefs who lacked inspiration in foreign surroundings.

The greatest number of chefs outside France were in the
United States, where Charles Ranhofer of Delmonico's took
the lead. Ranhofer had served royalty in Europe and had directed the grand balls of Napoleon III. In 1862 he decided to
make the United States his home and transplanted the sumptuous menus of the Second Empire to Delmonico's, already

noted for its French cuisine. As author of *The Epicurean*, a tasteful gathering of the best in *haute cuisine*, he lives on in gastronomy.

French cooking had its American admirers well before Ranhofer arrived. Thomas Jefferson and Benjamin Franklin enjoyed it in the eighteenth century. By 1835 Captain Marryat, an English visitor, reported, "In New York, at Delmonico's, the Globe Hotel, and the Astor House, you have excellent French cooking from the *carte*." Delmonico's menu was already unreservedly French, but an Astor House menu of 1835 mingling *Rouleau de veau jardinière, Fricandeau de veau aux épinards,* and *Côtelettes de mouton panée* with boiled codfish, roast pig, and mince pie suggests a dichotomy in the kitchen.

In America in the 1880s a hunger for French cooking gnawed at the newly rich. Americans who could not read a word of French wanted the menu cards on their elaborate tables written in French, and the dishes prepared by the best French chefs dollars could buy. French chefs had responded in sufficient numbers to the greenbacks dangled by American millionaires to warrant Societé branches in New York, Chicago, St. Louis, Philadelphia, Cincinnati, San Francisco, and Washington, where embassies were heavy employers.

Conspicuously absent were such bastions of older money as Boston, Charleston, and New Orleans. To Bostonians the commotion over French chefs was for the vulgar new-rich. Charleston and New Orleans, seeded by Frenchmen, took an independent direction, adding southern touches to their own versions of French cuisine prepared by turbaned black cooks.

One southern belle, Alva Smith of Mobile, Alabama, dispensed with all southern culinary pretensions when she came to New York as the bride of William K. Vanderbilt. Her husband lured chef Dugniol from the noted Paris restaurant Paillard "for a fabulous salary." With him in the kitchen Mrs. Vanderbilt wrestled the redoubtable Mrs. Astor, leader of New York society, to a draw, and crowned her achievements by marrying her daughter, Consuelo, to the Duke of Marlborough.

The "fabulous salary" paid Dugniol was rumored to be

about twenty thousand dollars a year, which probably included perquisites. "An A-1 chef's wages is one hundred dollars a month; he takes ten percent commission of the butcher, grocer, baker and milkman's bill. If he does not get it directly, he gets it indirectly," wrote Ward McAllister. For the less qualified chef the take decreased to five percent. The same wages and commissions were quoted in *Millionaire Households* (1903), a book designed to help new millionaires spend their money so that it cast the proper glow on them.

In his fatuous book about society, McAllister, who conceived the phrase describing New York's top society as *The Four Hundred*—"There are only about four hundred people [in New York] who are at ease in a ballroom"—described the coming of the French chef onto the American scene.

"About [1870] . . . a new era came in. . . . The French chef then literally, for the first time, made his appearance, and artistic dinners replaced the old-fashioned, solid repasts. [In New York at that time] there were not over three chefs in private families. It is now [1890] the exception not to find the man of fashion keeping a first-class chef or a famous *cordon bleu*." Famous or not, McAllister agreed with *L'Art Culinaire* about women cooks. "No woman, in my opinion, can give as finished a dinner as a man. There is always something in the dinner which has escaped her."

Few French chefs in America found American dishes worth passing along to readers of *L'Art Culinaire*, and continuously described their own inventions. Ernest Glass, an exception, translated American favorites into French. Fish chowder became *Bouille-abaisse Americaine*; buckwheat cakes became *Pannequets de sarrasin*; southern cornbread translated into *Pain de mais de sud*; and blueberry pie became *Tarte aux baies bleu*. Nonplussed when it came to rendering popovers in French, he settled for *Popovers de Boston*.

Alfred Suzanne made no attempt to translate England's Cocky Leeky, trifle, and Mulligatawny into French, though he carefully described how to prepare them. He preferred to discuss the English themselves in most of his dispatches, faintly scornful of their insular gastronomy but happy that many of his confrères were on hand to teach the English better ways. His summary of French chefs working in England in the 1880s revealed that most were in the employ of "the big hats of finance who, here as everywhere, will have only French chefs in their kitchens."

The four English Rothschild families led the list, which included Lords Brougham, Clarendon, Shrewsbury, Salisbury, and "The English Lucullus," Lord Sefton. The list expanded in "the Victorian nineties. Then," wrote the American Lucius Beebe, "it was said that the best chefs in France are in the kitchens of London." In good part, César Ritz and Auguste Escoffier brought this about when they came to London in 1889.

The Ritz Touch

*"Civilized man cannot live
without cooks."*

E. R. Bulwer-Lytton

The combination of César Ritz and Auguste Escoffier "was one of the most fortunate things that ever happened in either of the two men's lives," Marie Ritz wrote in *César Ritz, Host to the World,* her book about her husband. That remark invites no argument. The two were indispensable to each other. "Until [Ritz] met Escoffier he had not yet been able perfectly to apply his ideas . . . as to Escoffier, until he met Ritz no one had fully appreciated his talents nor given him full scope to exercise them."

Both men had infallible taste and an unerring instinct for what was appropriate. Ritz knew in his bones, how to create serene luxury that spread contentment among the guests. Escoffier had the same inborn feeling for the right combination of flavors and texture to gladden the palate.

"Both men delighted in simplicity," said Mrs. Ritz. "While Ritz was abolishing senseless ornaments and dust-collecting fabrics, Escoffier, in his kitchen realms, was abolishing use-

Pen and ink sketch of Cesar Ritz by Mercedes Cummings, 1979.

less and inedible garnishments, simplifying menus, simplifying sauces."

The association that brought the two men international fame began in Monte Carlo in 1884, but before that their careers had followed almost parallel paths. Both came from sturdy peasant stock. Escoffier, four years older than Ritz, was born in the tiny village of Villeneuve-Loubet in southern France at the foothills of the Alpes Maritime. Ritz came from an almost identical village in Switzerland—Niederwald, in the shadow of the Jungfrau.

Both were lads of thirteen when they began their careers and both were pushed into them by their fathers: Ritz as an apprentice wine steward in a small hotel in nearby Brig, Escoffier as an apprentice cook in the restaurant kitchen of his uncle, Jean Escoffier. Both lads preferred a career in the arts but adapted readily to the professions chosen for them.

In 1870, as yet unacquainted, they were within calling distance of each other in Paris; Escoffier as a *saucier* at the

Moulin Rouge, Ritz as a waiter at the equally elegant Café Voisin. When business in Paris restaurants went slack during the resort seasons, both young men found employment in resort hotels. But Escoffier repeatedly returned to Paris restaurants while Ritz gravitated to resort hotels. By 1880 both men had arrived at important posts, Escoffier as the manager of the Maison Chevet, Ritz as manager of the Grand National Hotel in Lucerne.

Ritz had been summoned to the Grand National in 1877 by its owner, Colonel Pfyffer d'Altishofen, to take over its management. The colonel had built a fine hotel, but as he knew little about running one the Grand National was in difficulty. Young Ritz was already known for resourcefulness demonstrated at the Rigi Kulm Hotel in Rigi, Switzerland. There, one cold wintry day when the heating system failed just as a large party on a luxury tour was expected for luncheon, he beguiled the guests by grouping them intimately around one table with a blazing fire to gaze at, hot bricks wrapped in flannel to keep their feet warm, and hot food that began with steaming soup and ended with *crêpes flambées* for dessert. He created warmth for the guests and a reputation for himself.

Making the Grand National profitable required more than illusory tricks, but as its manager Ritz soon built a reputation as an astute hotelier who had pumped life into a faltering hotel and established it as a major resort.

The Grand National's season was only July and August, but Ritz made every day count. The rest of the year, like most resort personnel, he followed the changing of the social guard at other resorts. From 1876 to 1879 he was manager, in turn, of the Hotel de Nice and the Hotel Victoria in San Remo on the Italian Riviera, and the Hotel des Iles Britannique in Menton.

It was fairly swift progress for a young man not yet thirty, but the restless, ambitious young Swiss was impatient to be on his own. The opportunity came in 1879 with a chance to participate in leasing Les Roches Noires, a hotel in Trouville on the Normandy coast. The limelight had begun to play on Trouville during the Second Empire when Empress Eugénie paid it frequent visits. Its future still seemed promising to

Ritz and his associate, a former colleague when both were at the Hôtel Splendide in Paris. The register of the Trouville hotel displayed such steady patrons as the Marquis de Talleyrand-Périgord, Prince de Sagan, Baron d'Erlanger, and an assortment of Rothschild barons; one, Baron Gustave, grumbled peevishly to Ritz about the high price charged for his room.

For the guests, the service and attention to detail that had already earned Ritz a reputation made the season a success. But Trouville's season was brief, and for the undercapitalized partners it was a disaster. Ritz's total savings were lost. The ill wind, however, blew Ritz toward Escoffier. In Trouville he met Jean Giroix, a chef who had worked with Escoffier at the Moulin Rouge and spoke of him to Ritz.

The Trouville venture had also upset Colonel Altishofen, who, with little advance notice, had been left without a manager just as the season was about to begin. But he was a forgiving fellow and a sensible one as well: Ritz was a valuable asset to his hotel. Altishofen welcomed Ritz back as summer manager and as a further gesture of forgiveness got him the post of manager of the Grand Hotel in Monte Carlo for the long Riviera season.

It is a question as to who was best served in this alliance—Ritz or the Grand. The Grand, recently bought by the Jungbluth family of hotelkeepers, was a faded belle, one of the first hotels built in Monte Carlo. Its competition was the newly built and luxurious Hôtel de Paris, radiant with youth and owned by the Sea Bathing Society, the group François Blanc had formed to operate the gambling casino. The casino's devoted following of English and continental aristocrats and rich Americans considered the Hôtel de Paris the only hotel to stay at and fought for accommodations there. The Grand had to be content with the overflow.

Ritz at once set about to change this situation, using the same lures that had served him so well elsewhere, the utmost in luxurious service and the finest cuisine obtainable. The Grand's chef, though adequate, could not meet the standards Ritz had in mind as part of his plan for reviving the hotel.

Ritz wasted no time. He knew Jean Giroix to be a fine chef with superior experience; furthermore he would be Ritz's own man. Giroix was brought to Monte Carlo and the duel between the Grand and the Hôtel de Paris was on.

The Grand's resurgence was soon felt by its rival. Word spread that the rooms had been elegantly refurbished, that the impeccable service was like having one's own personal staff at hand. And the food—irresistible! The Hôtel de Paris lost some of its guests to the Grand at once, among them the Irish impresario Richard d'Oyly Carte, whose interest in the renovated Grand was somewhat professional. Some day soon he hoped to build a similar hotel in London.

The biggest triumph was a visit from the Prince of Wales, who left Cannes to come to the Grand during Ritz's second season there, no doubt attracted by tales of its splendid cuisine. His arrival dinner, ordered to be "something light and interesting," was carefully planned. Ritz built it around Giroix's newly created *Volaille à la Derby*—a tender young chicken stuffed with rice, foie gras, and truffles, finished with a light touch of delicate cream sauce containing snips of foie gras and truffles to link it to its succulent stuffing. One suspects that the dish may have been originated at that time as a compliment to the Prince. The recipe, over Giroix's name, appeared the following year in *L'Art Culinaire*.

As the Grand made steady inroads into the guest list of the Hôtel de Paris, the board of the Sea Bathing Society summoned the managers, the Catalan brothers, to account for this irritating phenomenon. With incredible speed the Grand had become their archrival. To what was this sudden success due? Chiefly to its chef, was the managers' guess. Well, then—get him for *our* hotel, ordered the board. The Catalan brothers were desperate. The offer they promptly tendered Giroix was too tempting to resist. Giroix moved to the Hôtel de Paris.

Again Ritz acted quickly. Escoffier, at the Maison Maire, was the man he needed. He did not know him personally but knew from Giroix that he rejected the overblown style of the Carême school and created simple, elegant dishes, occasionally with a touch of his native Provence. The Jungbluths had heard favorable reports about his efficient kitchen management. It was enough. Ritz made Escoffier an offer well beyond the generous figure that had lured Giroix away, and at the height of the 1883-84 season Escoffier became *chef de cuisine* at the Grand Hotel in Monte Carlo.

The two men were instantly drawn to each other. "A perfect accord," Escoffier described it. "Our ideas and thoughts meshed exactly." Escoffier knew his value. As he matter-of-factly put it, "Ritz needed a *chef de cuisine* who fully understood the art of *grande cuisine* and who was familiar with restaurant service where one dined *à la carte*, a knowledge which I possessed."

In most hotels, even those that counted themselves luxurious, *table d'hôte* which offered little choice was still the rule. Ritz chose to run his dining room in the manner of the grand restaurant, but with few grand restaurants as yet in existence, there were not many chefs with experience in them. Escoffier's expertise in directing a kitchen geared to serving *à la carte* was indeed valuable.

It was soon apparent that once again a new hand ruled the Grand's kitchen. Now the talk went that Giroix had been replaced by an even better chef, who not only prepared innovative dishes to suit the mood and taste of each diner, but to suit the weather as well. From Escoffier's notes and articles, and his frequently expressed view that warm-weather foods should be light and easily digested, it is possible to imagine some temptations he would have produced: broiled duckling flanked by a salad of chilled sliced oranges; sautéed sweetbreads with crisp, chilled cucumbers in a cloud of remoulade sauce; cold pink rack of lamb in sparkling aspic, framed with spring vegetables. Of course hearty eaters could gorge themselves on heavy dishes if they chose to. The kitchen was at their disposal no matter how ill-advised their choice.

The first season Ritz and Escoffier worked together in Monte Carlo proved their excellence as a team. That summer Escoffier joined Ritz at the Grand National in Lucerne.

The Grand National, under Ritz's management, had become so popular that despite its enormous size it could have filled premises twice as large. Ritz had transformed it into a brilliant social center. Major and minor royalty flowed through the corridors bringing retainers and sycophants in their train. The clamor for reservations made a pleasant thunder in the ears of the management. It was hardly necessary to give a spur to the hotel's popularity at this time, with rooms available only to the most faithful of the hotel's following, but Ritz, with a shrewd eye to keeping it galloping for the future, inaugurated a weekly ball and cotillion. This developed into a social event that commanded extensive press coverage and attracted society from all over Europe. Americans too fought and bought their way into the coveted rooms; Vanderbilts and Morgans brought their families to enjoy the festivities and the bracing Swiss climate, and no doubt to survey the European marriage market.

Ritz and Escoffier, each alter ego to the other, continued to alternate between Monte Carlo and Lucerne, their reputations growing along with their mutual esteem. It was an ideal situation.

In 1887 the ideal situation was interrupted by a series of events that began with Ritz's marriage to Marie Beck, a member of a hotel-owning family that included her aunt, Mrs. Jungbluth, owner of the Grand in Monte Carlo. Marriage quickened Ritz's urge to have his own business; the sale of the Grand in Monte Carlo to new owners, followed almost immediately by the Lucerne hotel owner's transfer of its management to his sons, hastened Ritz into a decision to make his second attempt at independence.

In Baden-Baden a small municipally owned restaurant was put up for public sale. Among the friends Ritz had made there was the wealthy and influential Otto Kahn. Kahn maneuvered the sale to Ritz and put up part of the money himself. Propitiously, as if to fill in the months when Baden-Baden was inactive, the Hôtel du Provence in Cannes also came on the market. With Kahn's aid Ritz bought it and became the owner of two properties, which demanded his full attention and a tight hold on his purse. There was no place for Escoffier in this new undertaking.

Escoffier now commanded a salary far beyond the resources of Ritz's newly acquired properties. Even if Ritz had offered him a financial interest in the venture—which he did not—it is doubtful that Escoffier would have accepted. As a married man with two small sons, he probably felt more secure retaining his remunerative posts at the Grand National and the Grand. Regretfully Ritz and Escoffier separated.

Ritz's venture prospered immediately. Encouraged, he leased the small Minerva Hotel in Baden-Baden and notified his faithful following that the pampering they had come to expect of him was available in a new setting. The Prince of Wales responded with a visit, which was enough to bring on the familiar clamor for reservations. Without Escoffier to rely on, Ritz supervised the kitchen closely himself and worked with the chef, hoping for the day when he could afford a reunion with Escoffier.

A table d'hôte *in a resort town on the Riviera. Drawn by Charles Bertall, nineteenth century.*

An English
Impresario

"A dinner lubricates business."

Boswell

T he reunion of Ritz and Escoffier was brought about in 1889 by Richard d'Oyly Carte, the diminutive British impresario who had welded Gilbert and Sullivan into a similar partnership. D'Oyly Carte was forty-five, about the same age as Escoffier and Ritz, and as driving and ambitious as the first Napoleon, whom he resembled in stature.

After an early start in his twenties handling such clients as Adelina Patti and Charles Gounod, D'Oyly Carte had become manager of the Royalty Theatre in London. He soon saw that the longest queues formed at the box office for Offenbach operettas. If the public wanted lighthearted operetta, why depend only on Offenbach? Why not expand the supply? His reply to himself was to commission an original work by William Schwent Gilbert, a sour, choleric man paradoxically gifted with a knack for humorous writing. The eminent organist Arthur Sullivan agreed to do the music. The pair's first effort was *Trial by Jury*, which opened to great success in March 1875.

D'Oyly Carte was off and running. Soon he leased the Opéra Comique theatre in London, formed a small syndicate of backers, and organized a company to perform light opera. This formed the nucleus of the celebrated original Savoyard company. Dissension developed among the backers and D'Oyly Carte, along with Gilbert and Sullivan, withdrew from the original group and formed their own partnership.

The success of their productions surpassed D'Oyly Carte's optimistic expectations. The profits multiplied like jungle growth. D'Oyly Carte proposed investing some of the earnings to build a new theater, and in 1881 he opened the Savoy Theatre on a Thames riverfront site in the center of London, a property whose provenance dated back to a thirteenth-century Count Savoy.

With his theater venture firmly established, D'Oyly Carte's ambition now turned to the hotel industry. On his frequent trips to America to fight copyright infringements on Gilbert and Sullivan works, the ebullient impresario had noted the spread of luxury hotels in America. Again he asked himself a question. Why not a luxury hotel in London? He already had the perfect location for one; the land alongside the Savoy Theater.

D'Oyly Carte's imagination had been particularly fired by the new Palace Hotel in San Francisco. Its elegant dining room reminded him of the Grand's in Monte Carlo, where the team of Ritz and Escoffier was in brilliant command. On his next visit to Monte Carlo he sought out Ritz and spent hours talking to him about the hotel business, implying, though he made no direct offer at the time, that Ritz's talent for supplying luxury could lead to great success in London. "You'd make money hand over fist."

A hotel in England held no appeal for Ritz. England's early closing laws and Sunday prohibitions appeared to be insurmountable obstacles, and furthermore, better-class people still did not dine out in restaurants in England. Moreover, Ritz pointed out, he was well settled in the Monte Carlo and

Lucerne hotels. D'Oyly Carte did not press the point at the time but resolved that when he was ready Ritz and Escoffier would be on his team.

Three years after the Savoy Theater opened, D'Oyly Carte began work on the hotel. It would introduce such revolutionary innovations as electric lights throughout, and sixty-seven bathrooms for its two hundred and fifty rooms and suites. The Victoria Hotel, its closest rival, had four bathrooms—yes, four—for five hundred guests. D'Oyly Carte had noted that in America bathrooms were generously supplied. Americans, now traveling in great numbers to Europe, particularly to London, would surely welcome and patronize the hotel he had in mind.

Exactly as he had anticipated, Americans were on hand for the brilliant opening on August 6, 1889, of "The hotel de luxe of the world," as the opening advertisement of the Savoy Hotel proclaimed. The first gold sovereign received on opening day was tendered by a Chicagoan, Harry Rosenfeld, for a bottle of Moët et Chandon champagne. The menu paid Amer-

D'Oyly Carte, from the Spy cartoon.

icans the compliment of seeming to expect them by offering such typical American specialties as clams, terrapin, sweet corn, and pumpkin pie.

Everything about the new hotel was exciting; success was instantaneous; visitors to London clamored for reservations. But D'Oyly Carte was a cautious man. He recalled Ritz's objections to opening a hotel in London, his concern because Londoners did not dine out. For the Savoy Hotel to be a success the dining room would need local patronage. Visitors from other countries and from English cities might be sparse at times, and when bedrooms were not filled to capacity the dining room had to be. A man like Ritz, who had already turned two losing hotels into winners, would find an answer.

By this time Escoffier and Ritz had separated and Ritz was in Baden-Baden. D'Oyly Carte set out for the spa, ostensibly to rest and take the cure after the rigors of opening his new hotel. His only motive was to capture the aloof Ritz.

This time D'Oyly Carte's overtures were open and direct. Ritz remained indifferent. He would not leave Baden-Baden. D'Oyly Carte then tried another gambit. For a handsome fee would Ritz come to London for a brief stay as a consultant while the hotel was still in its opening bloom, to give his opinion of the operation? Well, why not, reasoned Ritz. He wanted to see the new hotel; he might even gain a few ideas by doing so.

"He [Ritz] returned from London in almost a fever of excitement," Marie Ritz wrote in her book. "Mr. Richard d'Oyly Carte was right. Now was the time to launch huge luxury hotels." Though he was accustomed to seeing wealth paraded with seeming indifference to its value, what Ritz saw in London was "simply indescribable . . . wealth pouring into the lap of London from Persia, India, Africa," and from America as well. "And what about the hotel itself?" Marie asked. It was truly a luxury hotel, Ritz told her. Beautifully situated on the Thames, with electricity throughout and more bathrooms than could be found in any European hotel. It was filled with wealthy visitors, he added. Marie looked at him questioningly.

"It will not succeed," Ritz said firmly. "Not under its present management . . . no imagination . . . no real grasp of organization . . . and an uninteresting cuisine."

Ritz told Escoffier the same story, as Escoffier's notes show. "The manager was a charming fellow but with no real knowledge of the hotel business and no connection with hotel-keepers of the continent." As for the chef, "Undoubtedly a fine chef, directly from a Baron Rothschild's kitchen, but he hasn't the least notion of how to run an *à la carte* restaurant kitchen."

Ritz's prophecy of failure was soon fulfilled. The hotel's share values dropped and the hotel operated at a deficit. D'Oyly Carte, backed by his board of directors, took urgent action. The flaws were obvious to him, as they were to Ritz. He needed Ritz, and Escoffier if Ritz could get him, to bail out the Savoy. At this point D'Oyly Carte was ready to meet any terms Ritz demanded.

They were tough. In addition to a munificent salary, Ritz demanded to be free half of the year to run his properties in Cannes and Baden-Baden. Agreed, said D'Oyly Carte and his beleaguered board.

The challenge of solving the Savoy's problems excited Ritz more than any previous venture. He was sure he could transform the hotel into D'Oyly Carte's vision if Escoffier could be persuaded to leave the Grand in Monte Carlo and join him. "I count on you to support me in this," he told Escoffier as he outlined his plans for the Savoy. "You must take charge of the kitchen." Escoffier's response is in his notes. "I foresaw a grand success and decided to follow Ritz to London."

Escoffier. A pen-and-ink sketch by Mercedes Cummings, 1979.

The
Grande Cuisine
Moves to London

*"The art of dining is no slight art,
the pleasure not a
slight pleasure."*

Montaigne

For nearly two hundred years English cooks bristled at the mention of French cooking, complained that "a French cook's head is stuffed with butter," "French cooking is a nauseous hodge-podge of kickshawes," and scolded their countrymen "who so fondly admire French messes." It is ironic that in the face of such determined resistance French cuisine spread to its fullest in England, and that Auguste Escoffier, one of its immortal architects, had his greatest success there.

When Escoffier and Ritz came to London in 1889 to guide the Savoy Hotel to success, a few ducal English homes already employed French chefs, but most upper-class English kitchens followed the practices of Alexis Soyer and Mrs. Beeton. Soyer, chef of the Reform Club, though a fine gentleman who took the needs of the working class to heart—his most successful publication was *Shilling Cookery for the Masses*—must be dismissed as a contributor to culinary advancement, English or otherwise. His methods, even his language, were unrelievedly oleaginous, as his instructions for preparing sole as fresh as possible bear out. "Five minutes ought not to elapse from the time [the sole] is swimming in water, till it is swimming in grease."

As for Mrs. Beeton, English housewives could thank her for clear, conscientious guidance in home and kitchen, but Mrs. Beeton's way led to predictable, unimaginative dining, ruled by the ubiquitous joint of mutton or beef. Her pages offered none of the dining enjoyment that traveled English people had savored in Paris restaurants and the Continent's resort hotels. It was not available in England except in a few aristocratic homes.

Ritz and Escoffier changed this when they introduced the *grande cuisine* to the English public. True, it was a limited public at first, but the effect spread quickly and was soon felt in most upper-class English kitchens. Little more than a decade later C. Herman Senn, a Swiss chef long at work in England, wrote in the preface of his Edwardian *New Century Cookery Book*, "It is now generally acknowledged that English cookery in its higher accomplishments has undergone a beneficial change [recently] and this improvement is chiefly due to a better knowledge and appreciation of French and other Continental recipes." Credit for this belonged in great part to the influence of Escoffier.

Ritz revolutionized hotel management with his methods at the Savoy. Escoffier did the same in the kitchen, introducing assembly-line procedures that anticipated the American efficiency engineer Frederick Winslow Taylor's time- and labor-saving methods. To prepare *Œufs Normande* (eggs with poached oysters and Normande sauce served in a *croustade*) the eggs would be cooked by the *entremettier* (responsible for all egg cookery, crêpes, fritters, and custards). The poached oysters would be prepared by the fish chef, the Normande sauce by the *saucier*. In minutes each chef would have his part of the dish ready and the eggs would proceed as if on an assembly line, without interruption or confusion. Other dishes were meanwhile prepared by the same hands for the same efficient consolidation. In the old system one chef would prepare the entire dish, requiring as much as thirty minutes.

Escoffier's kitchen ran with the precision of a modern plant, but the kitchen that greeted him at the Savoy his first day would have destroyed another chef. He was expected to choose a new kitchen brigade when he arrived, but a skeleton crew was to be retained temporarily; the others were given advance notice of dismissal.

"I'll never forget the unpleasant surprise that greeted me the day I arrived at the Savoy," he wrote. "The night before,

The Savoy Hotel.

all those who had been given their advance notice created a wild disorder in the kitchen and destroyed every bit of food we could possibly use. Not even a grain of salt was left. It was Sunday and all provision stores were closed. Luckily my good friend, director of the Charing Cross Hotel, was able to provide us with everything we needed. We met all demands without the least snag."

There may have been some snags that Escoffier chose not to recall, but the relaxed attitude that his remarks suggest was the way he approached most kitchen emergencies. Seemingly he was determined to be the reverse of the harried, temperamental chef. Though he is usually pictured in a *toque blanche* and white chef's coat, he more frequently dressed like a banker, moving through the kitchen in a frock coat, striped trousers, and carefully knotted cravat.

Escoffier and Ritz held to a basic rule: exquisite food must be served in exquisite dishes. A delicate fish mousse caressed with a mousseline sauce could repose only on equally delicate china, enhanced by gleaming silver and radiant crystal. What was not exquisite was promptly replaced.

The team found the Savoy dining room wanting when they took over. Though it had ornate paneled walls decorated by Whistler and lit by magnificent chandeliers, the lighting was unflattering to feminine diners. When table lamps with rosy silk shades were added, Escoffier noted, "The entire decor finally created a ravishing effect for the ladies it framed." It was a vital improvement. The reluctance of the English— especially English ladies—to dine in public restaurants was perhaps the most serious problem Ritz and Escoffier faced.

In his resort hotels Ritz had dealt with such resistance by creating the atmosphere of a home dining room, a grand home of course. This had now been accomplished at the Savoy. But the ladies continued to resist. In London, actresses, singers, *demimondaines,* and those few women who held themselves above convention were already visible in public places. Ladies did not wish to be confused with them. It was said at the time that any woman dining publicly with a man could be assumed not to be his wife. Until the Savoy became popular, even members of the Marlborough House set, the

racy British coterie of the Prince of Wales, did not often venture beyond their grand homes or private eating clubs.

But Ritz knew that marked changes had come over English high society, due greatly to the Prince's leadership. He also knew that a few carefully selected bellwethers could guide society to new pastures, and that Wales's circle was essential to the success of the Savoy. Lady Dudley, whose name often appears in the Prince's engagement diary as his companion for late supper, eventually took many of those suppers at the Savoy. Along with Lady de Grey and such social tigresses as the Duchess of Devonshire, leaders powerful enough to bridge their exclusive stratum to less conventional society, Lady Dudley gave the Savoy Hotel the authoritative imprimatur. The snobs followed, eager to be accepted as regulars in the Savoy dining room as it became the place to be seen.

Ritz carefully controlled the influx, feeding it like plasma into the veins of the dining room. *Demimondaines* were discouraged, or at least assigned with their escorts to the least conspicuous tables. "Reserved" cards held the most prominent tables for diners deemed worthy of a conspicuous location, whether or not they had indeed been reserved. It was a new ploy which became standard practice in all exclusive restaurants. *Exclusivity* was the guiding principle of the Savoy Hotel's restaurant, and under the protection of that word English ladies felt secure to appear there with masculine escorts.

Correct dress was mandatory. The Savoy's rule against

ladies wearing hats recalled a similar restriction by Beau Nash at Bath in the eighteenth century. The Beau banished aprons as unsuitable for the formal atmosphere he wished to maintain, though the aprons were merely accessories, like belts or scarves today, made of costly Alençon or Brussels lace. Nevertheless, to the Beau they were reminiscent of servants' attire. The Savoy ruled against head coverings on similar grounds: they belonged to daytime carriage promenading or shopping excursions. At that time hats *were* distracting, weighed down with whole birds, masses of ribbons, and enough flowers to fill a wash basin. Any head covering beyond a tiara or aigrettes had to be removed before a lady could enter the dining room.

Once admitted, subtle culinary flattery greeted them, delicate food and specialties bearing feminine names: *Perdrix Lady Clifford* (a partridge cooked in butter, then surrounded with sliced truffles and doused with brandy); *Coupe Emma Calvé* (pralined ice cream masked with cherries in kirsch and topped with a raspberry purée); *Fantasie de Marguerite* (a cheese soufflé given grand airs surrounded by tiny crawfish tails and sliced truffles).

For Queen Victoria's diamond jubilee, Escoffier created *Cherries Jubilee,* now served over vanilla ice cream, but originally calling only for cherries.

The best known of Escoffier's many dishes dedicated to his feminine following is probably *Pêche Melba.* Its origination has many versions, but the most accurate is surely Dame Melba's own. "I was lunching alone . . . particularly hungry, and was given a most excellent luncheon. Towards the end of it there arrived a little silver dish which was uncovered before me with the message that Mr. Escoffier had prepared it specially for me. And much as Eve tasted the first apple, I tasted the first *Pêche Melba* in the world.

"'It's delicious,' I said. 'Ask Mr. Escoffier what it is called.' Word came back that it had no name, but that Mr. Escoffier would be honored if he might call it *Pêche Melba.* I said that he might with the greatest of pleasure, and thought no more of it. But soon afterwards *Pêche Melba* was the rage in London." It spread like brush fire to America as well, clearly the inspiration for the American sundae, which appeared almost simultaneously. In Escoffier's obituary the *New York Times* said, "Pêche Melba is the feudal name for our democratic sundae."

An elegant dessert without a feminine dedication is *Fraises Romanoff*, devised by Escoffier to compliment visiting Russian royalty. This called for strawberries steeped in orange juice and curaçao, chilled, then blanketed in whipped cream just before serving. In the 1940s a Hollywood figure who operated Romanoff's restaurant and called himself "Prince Romanoff" claimed to have invented *Strawberries Romanoff*. As his preparation was identical to the recipe that appeared in Escoffier's *Guide Culinaire* (1902), the Hollywood gentleman's claim was as bogus as his title.

French was the language of the menu at the Savoy, as it had been in Monte Carlo and Lucerne. There Escoffier and Ritz had noticed that many English and American guests, faced with a menu in French, "did not understand it well and relied on the *maître d'* to order their dinner." When the same thing happened at the Savoy, Escoffier introduced another innovation. Why bother guests with a *carte* they could not understand, he reasoned, when what they sought was a dinner well planned from beginning to end, and they willingly relied on experts to provide it? Why not give them a choice of price ranges instead? He would plan a suitable dinner to fit it. The *prix fixe* dinner, ranging from twelve shillings, sixpence, to one guinea (twenty-one shillings), available to any party of four persons or more, was introduced at the Savoy.

The Savoy's *prix fixe* dinners were required to be ordered some hours in advance through the *maître d'*. A slip giving the host's name, number of guests, and hour of service was sent to the kitchen where Escoffier himself composed "*a menu à mon idée.*" A duplicate menu was kept on file under the host's name to avoid repetition at a future time. The innovation caught on at once; it was one of the many attractions that soon made the Savoy a popular rendezvous.

As success mounted the dining room introduced *le souper*

de l'opéra. The Savoy became the place to be seen after opera and theater. Couples promenaded through the halls and terraces each night, creating a dazzling spectacle that made public after-theater dining another feature of London social life.

Two major stumbling blocks still had to be removed. English law forbade public dining rooms to remain open after 11:00 P.M. and barred any service on Sunday. The hand of the Society for the Reformation of Manners, founded during the reign of Charles II, still lay heavy on England after two centuries. The society had sponsored "An act for the Better Observance of the Lord's Day Commonly called Sunday" that declared "drinking, gambling, swearing, and whoring," illegal on that day. What could be done about "whoring" is a moot question; but during the reign of Queen Anne the society managed to place temptation to drink well out of reach, at least in public places. To please the reformers the Queen "forbade the sale of even a cup of tea or chocolate on Sunday, lest stronger stuff be sold in seemingly innocent containers."

Ritz tolerated few obstacles. Antiquated laws that had outlived their usefulness were challenges to be met and overcome. To that end he enlisted the aid of Savoy patrons who were prominent in public life, among them Henry Labouchère, a leading liberal, and at the opposite end of the political spectrum, Lord Randolph Churchill, leader of the Conservative party, whose American wife, Jennie Jerome, and her American friends helped to bring cachet to the Savoy restaurant.

Apparently the time was right for a change in the laws governing hotels. Their review took place with astonishing rapidity and new interpretations quickly followed. "It was found that a hotel of the Savoy's class might actually keep its restaurant open until a half hour after midnight; and that Sunday dinner need not be prohibited," Marie Ritz wrote in her book about her husband.

Ralph Nevill reported in *The World of Fashion,* "After the opening of the 'Savoy' in the late eighties and nineties it became the smart thing to dine there on a Sunday evening—

OPERA SUPPER.

Consommé Riche au Marsala en tasse

Suprême de Sole Renaissance

Chapon à la Savoy

Jambon Ambassadrice

Chaud froid de Gibier St. Hubert
Salade Joyeuse

Compotier de Fruits
Gourmandises.

A Savoy supper menu.

and very agreeable it was . . . Everything was beautifully done and a number of celebrities were always present."

Ritz introduced still another innovation to sustain the gala mood and a flow of champagne, and to prolong the consumption of food: music during dinner. Johann Strauss and his orchestra, in the city for a series of concerts, was Ritz's inspired choice to launch this latest contribution to nighttime gaiety in London. Its great success soon caused restaurants and hotels far from the London scene to follow; music during dinner became so widespread that Henrici's, a fashionable restaurant in Chicago, built its reputation and success on the reverse approach, promising its patrons, "No orchestral din during dinner."

Both Escoffier and Ritz were deeply occupied guiding the Savoy Hotel to success and had little time for normal family life. This did not disturb resourceful Marie Ritz, who came from a family of hoteliers. She shared her husband's interests, understood his problems, and was by nature as gregarious and at ease with people as he was. She found London stimulating and exciting and enjoyed moving in London society.

Delphine, Escoffier's wife since 1878, was not so fortunate. The damp London climate disagreed with her. She was shy and found it painful to be with strangers, especially with people whose language she did not speak or understand well. Even Escoffier, after many years in England, spoke English haltingly though he eventually understood it well. When asked if he spoke English he would reply, "Yes!" then blithely launch a volley of French, sprinkling in a few words of English as he raced along.

Delphine made little effort at English. As an established poet, when she went about, which was rarely, she mingled with a few French intellectuals who lived in London. The Escoffier's two young sons and a daughter occupied her days. Occasionally her poems, signed with her maiden name, Daffis, appeared in *La Chronique*, a French journal published in London, but few Londoners outside her tight little French circle knew the name of Delphine Daffis.

Escoffier was another matter. Not only the rich and select patrons of the Savoy dining room, but many who never expected to be inside it, knew his name. It appeared frequently in accounts of social affairs at the hotel. The astute D'Oyly Carte, aware of the cuisine's importance to the Savoy's fame, saw to that.

When Delphine's health began to fail noticeably, Escoffier bought a small villa outside Monte Carlo where he settled the family. After that he became more of a visitor than a member of it until his retirement in 1919. London also saw less of him as he and Ritz expanded their operations in response to the growing popularity of travel.

The
Grande Cuisine
Travels

"At the dinner table no one should be bashful."
Plautus

"Y ou must take along your own knife and fork, or run the risk of losing your dinner," an eighteenth-century guidebook warned affluent young gentlemen setting out on the Grand Tour to complete their education. Inns supplied food all right, but rarely supplied the tools for consuming it.

By the 1860s inns supplied cutlery, and guidebooks dealt only with the specifics of what to see and how to get there. Many voyagers still pursued a Grand Tour for cultural enrichment or followed their social pack to resorts, but the majority of the travelers were now that new nineteenth-century phenomenon—tourists.

Tourism, the creation of Thomas Cook, had its unlikely genesis in England's Temperance movement, which began in 1841. Cook, a deeply religious Baptist, was one of its leading spirits and produced Temperance tracts and literature in his print shop. When it was decided to hold a big open-air meeting in the town of Leicester, some ten miles from Cook's home town, he was appointed to make arrangements for the journey for his townspeople. Railroads had begun to move passengers only a year earlier; before that they had moved coal. The fares were very high and Cook's contingent decided to walk the distance. Then the idea struck Cook that the Midland Counties Railway Company might be willing to run a special train at a reduced rate, as indeed they were. By this arrangement some three hundred people were taken to and from the meeting.

The train moved at walking pace, observing the "red flag law," which required a man carrying a red flag to precede all moving vehicles, to wave aside unwary pedestrians. Cook's account nevertheless managed to convey a feeling of speed. "The party rode the enormous distance of eleven miles and back for a shilling . . . people crowded the streets, filled the windows, covered the house-tops and cheered us along the line . . . thus was struck the keynote of my excursions."

In 1855 Cook's first excursion took English travelers across the channel to the Paris Exposition. A conducted tour to other capitals soon followed, with meals and lodging included—the forerunner of modern package tours.

By 1890 what began as an excursion to a Temperance meeting had grown into an enterprise that deposited crowds of travelers on the landscapes of Europe and North Africa, and earned Cook a crusty reproof in the press.

To travelers of the privileged class, who looked upon visits to Europe's cultural centers as their exclusive right, the flocks of twittering schoolteachers and retired army subalterns with

Pen and ink drawing by Charles Bertall.

their drab wives seemed invaders on a par with Ghengis Khan.

The Savoy Company and César Ritz, whose agreement with the Savoy Company allowed him to follow his personal interests for six months of the year, saw them differently. This new breed of travelers represented profit, not in themselves but in luxury hotels that could be built to protect the privileged and monied from them.

Ritz now served two masters: the Savoy Company and his own Ritz Development Company, formed with the backing of wealthy friends "to open hotels from Cairo to Johannesburg." Both groups saw in the capacity bookings of the Savoy a need for more hotels of its caliber in London and all over Europe, to accommodate millionaires eager to travel like sultans. Often such travelers brought along their own staffs of servants, who also had to be fed and lodged.

Some betrayed the newness of their wealth with their vulgarities. Barney Barnato, once of the London slums, then a street juggler in Johannesburg, and finally a partner of Cecil Rhodes and a governor of the DeBeers diamond mines, was singled out by the *Spectator* as "the commonest millionaire," for his habit of toting around a bag of diamonds which he would empty onto a table top to delight his guests. Diners at the Savoy were often treated to the sight.

Common or otherwise, millionaires crowded the Savoy and vainly sought similar hotels on their travels to other cities. In the early 1890s few hotels in Europe could be classified as deluxe. Some claimed the distinction, but fell well below the standards established by the Savoy, especially in their dining rooms, usually *table d'hôte* and maintained primarily for the convenience of lodgers. Away from the Savoy, the wealthiest traveler could do little better than the budget-bound tourist in obtaining lodging. But he could dine well if he took the train.

Luxurious dining first came to the railroads when Wagon-Lits were introduced in 1875. These counterparts of America's Pullman cars offered travelers restless sleep, but compensated with grand dining, proudly hailed in the first issue of *L'Art Culinaire* as another milestone in French cuisine. "To give an idea of the pleasure of dining in these 'wagon restaurants' and what one may have at the table, here is a menu executed by one of our colleagues, M. Arbeault, chef on the Orient Express."

Potage printanier
(Vegetable soup)
Bouchées Monglas, thon, salad d'anchovies, etc. . . .
(Tiny patty shells filled with foie gras, pickled tongue, truffles, and mushrooms in Madeira sauce, tuna, anchovy salad, and more)
Saumon, sauce hollandaise
Filet de bœuf à la Nivernaise
(Filet of beef garnished with small glazed onions and carrots)
Suprême de poularde financière
(Chicken breasts stuffed with chicken and truffle forcemeat, poached, garnished with Madeira sauce and truffles)
Jambon d'York aux épinards
(York ham with spinach)
Punch à la romaine
(Sherbet of champagne, orange and lemon juice, and stiffly beaten egg whites and sugar, served to "clear the palate")
Dindonneaux bardes
(Young turkey, roasted covered with bacon
to retain moistness)
Salade de saison
Pâté de fois gras aux truffes, buisson de crustacés
(A pyramid or "bush" of shellfish, perhaps surmounted by a dish of foie gras)
Petits pois à la Francaise, asperges sauce crême
(two favorite French vegetables)
Moka napolitain
(coffee? Napoleon pastry?)
Pâtisserie Montées

Travelers found the Wagon-Lits superior to many European hotels. Italian hotels were said to be the worst. Though some were reminiscent of palaces, with their expanses of marble

A Wagon-Lits *dining car.*

and lofty ceilings, travelers complained that their palatial splendor had to be shared with bedbugs and fleas. The food, from all reports, was as disappointing as Montaigne had found it in the sixteenth century.

Nevertheless, wealthy travelers and pennywise tourists alike were magnetized by the allure of Italy, especially Rome. The Savoy Company made that city its first target for expansion. In 1893, under César Ritz's direction, the Grand Hotel was opened with electricity throughout, an abundance of bathrooms on each floor and private ones for the suites, and an elegant dining room featuring an extravagant *à la carte* French menu. Escoffier came from London to establish the kitchen and was met with a repetition of the turmoil that had greeted him on his first day at the Savoy: this time a mutinous staff. "I was accustomed to working with a French staff," he explained in his notes. "The Italians would accept only their own countrymen in the kitchen . . ." His solution was as simple as his laconic description of it. "I solved it by making the brigade half-French and half-Italian."

Five thousand guests and Italian society in full strength attended the opening reception and exclaimed over the sumptuous buffet prepared in a kitchen now calm as a dovecote. As he had done in London, Ritz altered deep-rooted traditions in Rome. Ladies of Roman society who had previously shunned public appearances now dined and danced at the new hotel and attended its gala dinners and balls.

Ritz and the Savoy Company next planned a second London hotel on a site where a former butler, Claridge, had operated a cluster of private homes exclusively for visiting nobility and royalty. When these plans were complete, Ritz turned to Paris with a project for the Ritz Development Company.

For all its reputation as the most beautiful city in the world, with its glorious buildings, sweeping boulevards, opera, theaters and renowned restaurants, Paris received travelers like unwanted guests. Hotels supplied few of the luxuries sought by wealthy visitors. Private bathrooms were unheard of. The Hôtel Bristol, the most luxurious hotel in Paris before the Hôtel Ritz was built, had one bathroom to each floor, but did not object if guests ordered their own bath from a bath-at-home service, which carted tub, tanks of hot water, and all other necessities for a pleasant soak, across town to the hotel. The Prince of Wales resorted to this service when stopping at the Bristol, before the Ritz was built.

Dining facilities in hotels were limited or nonexistent. There were many restaurants but surprisingly few had been added to the list of those acclaimed. The best chefs were employed in private homes.

César Ritz itched for conquest. He saw Paris as the perfect location for the first hotel to bear his name, one he would build himself to embody his ideal of an elegant, exclusive hotel. Outwardly it would be unobtrusive, inside it would be luxurious beyond any yet built, with lavishly appointed suites, spacious private rooms, bathrooms for nearly all rooms; and it would have a restaurant in the grand tradition.

Had he been given a choice of all Paris, very likely he would have chosen the building that now became available. It had the appearance of a private home and stood in the impressive Place Vendôme, at the very heart of Paris, modestly joined to its neighbors on both sides. Ritz's backers said no. The building was too small, the price for it too high.

Ritz, the perfectionist of all time, was not to be dissuaded from a choice he judged to be flawless. He found other backers, headed by Marnier Lopostolle, inventor of the cordial Grand Marnier, which Ritz had named half-derisively when the pompous little man was discussing possible names for it. "Why not call it Grand Marnier?" Ritz joked. Lapostolle did just that and his gratitude knew no bounds. He happily lent Ritz the money to option the Place Vêndome property.

By 1898, in less than two years, the Hôtel Ritz was ready for occupancy. The seventeenth-century façade of the building had been left undisturbed, indeed the French authorities would have insisted on it. The interior of the hotel had been furnished to conform to the period. The furniture, copied from Louis XIV and Louis XV museum pieces, had all been specially built; the upholstery and drapery fabrics had been specially woven. The spell of the *ancien régime* lingered in every corner of the hotel.

To emphasize the feeling of a private home that Ritz meant to convey, each room was furnished differently, as if a personal owner had assembled it. In the dining room of the hotel, with its opulent silver by Cristofle and crystal by Bacarat, the same impression of individual taste at work suggested an unseen host awaiting his guests.

But no matter how perfect furnishings and decoration César Ritz knew that the success of his ideal hotel "depended not on these things, but rather on the cuisine, which must be excellent, and the staff, which must give perfection in service."

The *grande cuisine* traveled back to its homeland when Escoffier came from London to plan the kitchen of the Hôtel Ritz and remained to direct it during the opening months. A reporter expecting to find in it the most modern cooking equipment (a French chef at a private club in Sioux City, Iowa, had installed an electric stove in 1892, according to

L'Art Culinaire) was astonished to see only wood-burning and coke-burning stoves. "What! No gas or electricity?" he exclaimed. Escoffier showed him that both were present: a gas ring that burned constantly under the simmering pot of essential meat stock for sauces, and electric lights over stoves and work tables. For cooking Escoffier used only wood and coke. In his opinion only these fuels could produce the intense but slow-burning heat needed for fine cuisine. (Some small restaurants with flair still use wood and coal. A modest little Roman restaurant produced a distinguished shrimp dish worthy of the haughtiest cuisine on its coal-burning stove. "It wouldn't be the same with gas," the chef insisted.)

There was never any question of the success of the hotel's cuisine in Ritz's mind. It could compare with, and in some cases exceed, the best that Paris could offer. But how to attract diners to eat it was the problem that now confronted him. Though the gala Hôtel Ritz opening had brought out the choicest names in the Almanac de Gotha and Burke's peerage, Ritz soon realized that he faced the same difficulties he had met in London. While restaurants had long been popular with Frenchmen, patronized by bourgeois families and some of the less conventional members of the *haute monde*, the innermost circle of exclusive society had held itself apart and shunned public dining.

In its privacy, exclusive Parisian society dined in princely magnificence. Boni de Castellane, married to the American heiress Anna Gould, habitually entertained thirty guests at dinner with a footman for each guest. (Mary Pickford and Douglas Fairbanks provided the same luxury at Pickfair on occasion.) Rodman Wanamaker of the department store family, who lived for a while in Paris and mingled in its exclusive society, gave one dinner extravagant enough to be noted by both *Figaro* and *L'Art Culinaire*. For this entertainment a fleet of carriages collected the guests. At dinner Wanamaker surpassed de Castellane by not only providing a footman for each guest, but duplicating the entire menu, intact, for each one: a whole leg of lamb, a whole salmon, a whole fowl, as well as all other dishes in their entirety. The dinner concluded with a "grab bag" circulated around the table. Each guest dipped into it for a jeweled souvenir—cuff links for the gentlemen, brooches for the ladies.

Fortunately for Ritz and the future of his hotel, most Americans in Paris were not residents with their own establishments. Along with visitors from England and elsewhere, enough of them soon filled the dining room to quiet Ritz's concern. And as the hotel became the scene of lavish entertainments attended by de Castellane and other bellwethers, Parisian society gradually followed.

Soon after the Paris opening a rupture occurred between Ritz and the Savoy Company. This caused Ritz to terminate any further connection with the Savoy hotels and left him free to concentrate on the affairs of the Ritz Development Company and its next project, the Carlton hotel in London.

Each hotel evidently had its own board of directors and backers. With the Paris success to point to, it was an easy matter to find backers for the Carlton venture, and to establish a forceful board of directors that included the socially visible Lord de Grey, close friend of the Prince of Wales, and Harry Higgins, a guiding hand of the Covent Grand Opera Company.

"Luxury hotels were popping up like mushrooms everywhere in London," Madame Ritz wrote. The Carlton Company, eager to get its hotel underway—especially as the Savoy group was hurrying to complete Claridge's and starting a large annex to the Savoy—bought a building under construction. It was still an empty shell; Ritz could fill it as he chose.By all accounts, when the Carlton was completed it was the most modern hotel in London up to that time.

It exceeded all its competitors in the numerous and palatial private bathrooms which by now were the hallmark of any hotel under Ritz's wing. The same meticulous attention to detail that had made the furnishings of the Paris Ritz so distinctive had been paid to the rooms at the Carlton. Graceful Adam and elegant Georgian furniture gave the rooms a manor-house look. The "Ritz touch" became a phrase and a symbol of quality. Unfortunately for Ritz, he was unable to enjoy his latest success for very long. The merciless pace he had set himself for so many years brought on a nervous collapse and he was soon forced to retire.

Escoffier now made the Carlton his headquarters. When the Prince of Wales took a table in the dining room, an unheard-of precedent since he usually dined in one of the private rooms, the event was noted by London society and in the press. Madame Ritz saw it as an accolade, "It meant that the Carlton was the fashionable center of London." Seemingly she was correct. To quote *Punch*'s view when it later wrote of Edwardian society, "It was the Carlton, whose restaurant became the most fashionable."

Escoffier came in for his share of attention from the press. Lieutenant Colonel Newnham-Davis, England's version of a Brillat-Savarin and noted for his many articles on gastronomy, declared at the time, "Had [Escoffier] been a man of the pen and not a man of the spoon, he would have been a poet."

J. P. Morgan observed with interest the popularity of the Carlton and the praise heaped on Escoffier, and concluded that what succeeded on land could be put to use at sea. Morgan now controlled the Hamburg-Amerika line, and had temporarily wrested supremacy of the ocean lanes from Cunard. When Cunard's new *Campania* was launched, with a first-class dining room that could seat four hundred and thirty at one sitting, Morgan saw shipboard dining rooms as another field for combat and took the *grande cuisine* to sea.

Escoffier was engaged to help plan the first-class dining room of Hamburg-Amerika's new ship, the *Amerika*. Capitalizing on the renown of the chef, the Ritz Company, and the Carlton's dining room, the *Amerika*'s first-class dining room was called a Ritz-Carlton restaurant. Like all Ritz dining rooms it offered *à la carte* service, an innovation on ships. Previously all passengers, including first-class, had been bound to a *table d'hôte* menu. The huge success of this innovation caused Hamburg-Amerika to open Ritz-Carlton restaurants on its other liners. All were staffed with trainees from Escoffier's Carlton kitchen. Dining became a principal lure of ocean travel.

Learning
from a Master

*"A master cook! Why he is
the man of men."*

Ben Jonson

I t is fitting to conclude this book with Escoffier.
His name and influence still dominate classic
and *haute* or *grande cuisine*, which he skillfully blended in his
Guide Culinaire. Few professional kitchens are without a copy,
and while other excellent works have been produced, none
has superseded the *Guide* as an authority. It takes its place
alongside the works of La Varenne and Carême as one of the
supporting pillars of French cuisine.

In philosophy and method Escoffier was closer to La Varenne than to Carême. He stripped away many of the excesses
that had grown out of the Carême school, and early in his
career cried out against its "crowded, superfluous embellish-
ments . . . *socles, hâtelets, bordures.*" Even more important, he
recognized the changing times as his career proceeded, and
the need for chefs to deal with these changes.

"We must carry culinary simplicity to its outer borders," he
said. "The hectic times we live in demand it." He was all too

Charles Auguste Escoffier at the turn of the century.

aware that for many people "eating has become a necessary labor, instead of the pleasure it once was." The haste with which food was consumed and the increasing demand for rapid service dismayed and worried him. Faced with these demands, chefs had no choice but to comply, but what about the diners? How were their digestive systems to survive such abuse? Escoffier's answer was, "We chefs must reduce the harmful consequences of such attitudes by preparing lighter, more easily digested foods for stomachs exposed to the tensions and pressures of today. At the same time we must add savoury and nutritious value to our dishes."

Even in such grand restaurants as he was accustomed to, "radical changes" were required in the menus and service, and in the cooking itself. In his matter-of-fact way he acknowledged, "Circumstances ordained that I should manage the kitchens of the two establishments which have done the most to bring about [these changes]." In the kitchens of the Savoy and Carlton hotels he set his stamp on modern French cuisine through the young chefs he trained there. Eventually the Carlton became his main school.

By comparison with the laborious methods of his predecessors, Escoffier's methods seem elementary, but the results were immensely appealing. Just as he could describe a culinary method in a few concise sentences, he could create a ravishing dish with little effort. His fruit desserts are examples of the easy way he achieved his effects.

He may not have been aware of vitamins, but instinct led him to use methods that preserved the natural nutrients. He favored cooking methods that preserved the natural savor and appearance of food. "Spinach, peas, green beans and green vegetables in general, should be quickly cooked to preserve their chlorophyl," he instructed. For roasting he preferred the open spit to the oven because the natural juices, falling into a drip pan, were unmixed with the steam generated in a closed oven. "The *integralité* of the meat was thus preserved."

He was always on the alert to discover new methods and new variations in cookery. When he came across new dishes that *"fait l'eau m'en venait à la bouche"* (made my mouth water), a phrase that came often from his pen, he shared them with his readers in *Le Carnet d'Epicure*, a French publication he helped to found in London about 1910. (It was discontinued when World War I began.) In its pages he also shared his abiding love for the simple Provençal dishes of his youth by bringing his favorites to the attention of his readers.

The simplicity he preferred in cooking was typical of Escoffier himself. He was unpretentious, friendly, never pompous, easy to approach, and as plain as the sauces he favored. Yes, plain sauces. It is a mistake to link Escoffier to rich sauces and dishes overwhelmed by them, as if this were his stamp. He used sauces, of course, if a dish required them. He recognized their importance in the grand scope of the cuisine. But often he returned to La Varenne's simple method, using the juices that escaped from the food in cooking and reducing them for a sauce base.

If thickening was needed pure starch was his answer, not flour. "Remember that starch is the only element in flour that makes it thicken," he pointed out. Pure starch, arrowroot, cornstarch, or potato starch would "accomplish the same purpose but give a better result," he said, predicting that the time would come when flour as a thickening agent would be discarded.

Eugene Herbodeaux, an Escoffier trainee and co-author of his biography, *G.A. Escoffier*, could still recall at age eighty-five his first experience as a young *saucier* in the Carlton kitchen under Escoffier. Escoffier passed Herbodeaux's station, paused, saw that the *saucier* was thickening his roux with flour. Abruptly he lifted the pan from the stove and dumped its contents into a nearby bucket. "Forget everything you think you know about sauces," he commanded. "I will teach you *my* ways." Herbodeaux did learn Escoffier's ways and transmitted them to other young chefs.

Escoffier was a born teacher with an insatiable urge to share his knowledge. Whenever his current brigade of chefs was schooled to his satisfaction he lectured to English housewives, mainly trying to persuade them to use the round-bottomed French *poêle* instead of a flat-bottomed

LES GRANDS MENUS

GRAND HOTEL RITZ

Crevettes

Consommé Dame Blanche

Mousseline de Saumon au Paprika

Filets de Poulets au Beurre Noisette

Artichauts fines herbes

Selle d'Agneau a la Provençale

Délices de Cailles

Neige au Champagne

Ortolans au suc d'Ananas

Salade Rachel

Aubergines a la Grecque

Pêches flambées

Belle de Nuit (Glace)

Friandises

A. ESCOFFIER

"fraying pan." He never could learn to say frying pan. He would demonstrate the versatility of the *poêle* by preparing an entire meal in it: tomato soup *à la provençale*, sole *meunière*, noisettes of lamb with herbs, larks, or other small birds *à la bonne femme*, and for dessert, *crêpes au sucre*.

He found the housewives responsive and disagreed with his French contemporaries who considered English female cooks inept in the kitchen. "I compliment the ladies of England for their excellent cooking," he told an audience. Rosa Lewis, the noted professional cook of the Edwardian period (re-created for television audiences as Louisa Trotter in *The Duchess of Duke Street*), went a step further. "I think any woman cooks better than any man," she said, but on second thought exempted the chefs of France from this sweeping pronouncement. "France is the land of wonderful chefs," she admitted. "Escoffier is one of the greatest . . . in the world . . . a great gentleman and a great artist, very charitable and beloved and known by the whole of France." In a final burst of praise she added, "I learned a lot from Escoffier and I owe a great deal to him."

It is unlikely that Rosa or any other female ever worked alongside Escoffier, but his male trainees were just as admiring. From Escoffier's kitchens they fanned out all over the world, many of them to America.

Louis Diat, *chef de cuisine* of the Ritz-Carlton hotel when it opened in New York, was trained at the London Carlton, then sent to the London Ritz by Escoffier and from there to the Ritz-Carlton in New York.

Diat's *Crème Vichysoisse* is an excellent example of the simple, creative touches Escoffier sponsored, practiced, and encouraged his trainees to employ. By the simple addition of heavy cream and a garnish of chopped chives to the potato and leek soup of bourgeois French kitchens, an *haute cuisine* dish was created.

Escoffier kept in touch with many of his trainees long after they had gained recognition on their own, continuing to advise them as he did Charles Scotto, said to have been his favorite pupil. Scotto was *chef de cuisine* of Escoffier's first floating Ritz-Carlton restaurant on the Hamburg-Amerika line. In 1930, when Scotto was appointed *chef de cuisine* of the Hotel Pierre in New York, a coveted post that brought with it an annual salary of $35,000, Escoffier sailed over to attend the opening and continued their lengthy correspondence until his death.

Louis P. DeGouy, another Escoffier trainee, became known to numerous American gastronomes as food editor of *Gourmet* magazine. His *Gold Cook Book* is a suitable monument to an outstanding chef.

Many trainees entered private homes at munificent salaries. Joseph Donon is probably the most illustrious. In a 1962 article in the *New Yorker* he was referred to as "the most famous and very likely the richest private chef in the world."

As a beginning *sous-chef* of seventeen, Donon was unexpectedly called on to prepare a luncheon for his employer, the Marquis Panisse-Passis, and a guest. After the successful meal the pleased Marquis introduced the young chef to his guest, who turned out to be Escoffier. "If you're ever in London come and see me," Escoffier said graciously. Donon took him at his word, went to London to join the Carlton's brigade of seventy chefs, and remained there for five years, until he was required to enter the army for training.

When Donon's conscription period ended he returned to the Carlton. A dinner for twenty that he prepared for Henry Clay Frick resulted in an invitation from that wealthy gentleman to come to America as his chef. From Frick's home Donon went to the kitchen of Mrs. Hamilton Twombly, youngest daughter of William H. Vanderbilt. Unlike many high-salaried private chefs who vanished into limbo, Donon remains visible as one of the organizers of the gastronomic society Les Amis d'Escoffier. His excellent cookbook, *Classic French Cooking*, has secured his fame.

Donon is now a hearty, energetic fellow of ninety. Herbodeaux, nearly ninety, is still healthy and active in Nice. Another spry nonogenarian and former trainee of Escoffier, Andre Layet, who cheerfully admits, "I never created anything," is retired in Villeneuve-Loubet, where he and Escoffier were born. Escoffier also lived into his nineties.

The vigorous old age of these men is matched by that of many other creative people and says much for the regenerating quality of creativity. Creativity demands constant replenishment. In many of the arts, cookery certainly among them, the artist constantly searches for new springs to tap and is renewed by them. The painter, musician, conductor, or writer, however, can rarely transmit his talent to others as directly as a chef can, if he chooses to.

More than any chef before or since, Escoffier chose to point the way for others, and he was awarded the Légion d'Honneur for his efforts. At the time of his death the *New York Times* said, "At least two hundred chefs were trained by him personally." This figure did not include many who chose to enter other fields after training under Escoffier—for example Ho Chi Minh, the late president of North Vietnam, who was a trainee in the Carlton kitchen when Herbodeaux was a *saucier* there.

Two thousand chefs made widening ripples as they trained others in what they had learned and what they had invented. This was Escoffier's intention. In his introduction to his monumental *Guide Culinaire*, completed with the collaboration of his friends Phileas Gilbert and Emile Fetu and first published in 1902, he said, "While this volume contains almost five thousand formulas, I don't consider this *Guide* complete. What may be considered complete today may not be so tomorrow, for each day progress gives birth to new formulas.

Spoken like a true leader of French cuisine. Let all who delight in good eating say Amen.

Recipes from the Age of La Varenne

Pastry Shells   inspired by early *abaisses* and *tourtes*.

Pastry containers were the vogue in the seventeenth and eighteenth centuries but usually were used to hold ragouts of fish or meat. Here are pastry containers for desserts that can be eaten along with the ice cream or mousse they are to contain.

The pastry is shaped over the *back* of a baking mold and is most effective done on a scallop shell.

Cream together ½ cup shortening or butter with 1 cup sugar. When fluffy add 1 beaten egg and ½ teaspoon *each* of almond and vanilla extract. Combine 2 cups sifted flour, 1 teaspoon baking powder, and ¼ teaspoon salt and add to the creamed ingredients. Mix thoroughly. Chill overnight or at least six hours.

Grease the backs of the scallop shells. Pinch off a small quantity of dough for each shell, enough to cover it thinly. Make a ball of the dough and roll out thin on a lightly floured board. Shape the dough over the shell and cut away surplus.

Prick well with a fork and bake at 350° 10 minutes or until the shells are lightly browned. Cool slightly before removing and ease off carefully. Strawberry ice cream with strawberry sauce makes a great show in these shells.

Poitrine de veau farcis   La Varenne
(stuffed breast of veal)

La Varenne's breast of veal was made almost exactly as it is today, and his instructions closely follow professional manuals of today. Our additions are in brackets.

"Choose a fine white breast of veal. Bone it, then soak it in cold water while you prepare a stuffing: Take some forcemeat [grind up veal scraps or sausage], bread crumbs [soak 2 slices of bread, crusts removed, in milk; squeeze dry], chopped mushrooms, chopped minced onion [sauté first], capers [optional], egg yolks [or 1 or 2 whole eggs, depending on quantity of stuffing], mix all together and season well [salt, pepper, ¼ teaspoon thyme and/or rosemary]. This accomplished, stuff the breast with it, fasten it with skewers or sew it and braise until tender [covered, at 300° for 25 to 30 minutes per pound]. If you roast it [he meant roast on a spit] don't stuff it as much as for braising." We recommend braising.

Potage de jaret de veau   La Varenne
(potted veal shanks)

This ancient dish appears in both Italian and French early cookery. In Italian cuisine it is called *osso buco*. Here is La Varenne's recipe, as proof that in his day the dish had a French accent.

Have the shanks cut into rounds 2½ inches thick. Season them with salt and pepper, and brown them along with a sliced onion and some shallots. (La Varenne did this in butter.) When browned, place the veal and onions in a casserole with a tight cover; add bouillon to about 1 inch deep. Bring the bouillon to the boil, skim if necessary, then reduce the

heat, cover the casserole, and simmer gently for about 1½ hours. After 1 hour, add some raw mushrooms sliced fairly thick, and some heads of endive (Belgian endive; La Varenne specified one head per serving). If it appears that the shanks will need to cook more than 30 minutes longer, delay adding the mushrooms and endive until this point is reached. Serve the shanks surrounded by fresh garden vegetables.

Lentilles fricassee	from *Les Dons de Comus*,
(cooked lentils)	Marin

Wash the lentils and cover amply with water; they will swell. Add a sliced onion and a bay leaf to the pot. Bring to the boil, then lower heat and simmer gently for about 35 minutes or until lentils are tender but not too soft. Drain and cool completely.

Slice and sauté a large onion in butter until soft and beginning to turn color. Add the lentils, salt, pepper, some savory (the perfect herb for all dried legumes and beans), and some julienne strips of ham. Combine gently to avoid mashing the lentils. At the end add 1 or 2 tablespoons of vinegar. Serve warm as a side dish.

Lentilles a l'huile   from *Les Dons de Comus,*
(lentil salad)   Marin

Soak and simmer the lentils as in *lentilles fricassee*. When cool refrigerate them. To serve add salt, freshly ground black pepper, chopped chives, oil and vinegar, and toss as for a salad. (Marin directed that they be served in a glass bowl.) Garnish with tiny fried bread croutons. (We recommend crisp hot crumbled bacon as a finishing touch.)

Oye à la moutarde   Marin
(goose with mustard)

This will work just as well with duck as with goose. Season a duck inside and out. In the cavity place a medium sliced onion, 3 shallots, 2 tablespoons fresh chopped basil or 1 tablespoon dried, and 1 tablespoon butter kneaded with 1 tablespoon flour (*beurre manie*).

Truss the duck and place it on a rack in a roasting pan in a preheated oven (350°). Allow 20 to 25 minutes per pound. After 20 minutes puncture the duck in fatty places to encourage the fat to run out. Drain off fat as it accumulates and add a bit of water to the bottom of the pan to avoid scorching. At intervals baste with the pan juices if the duck appears to need it.

When duck is tender and as crisp as you wish, remove it from the pan, pour off all remaining fat, remove the onion, basil, etc., from the duck's cavity and place this in the roasting pan. Pour in some chicken stock (enough to make the quantity of sauce desired). Cook and stir for 1 minute over brisk heat, then lower heat and reduce sauce by one third. Strain through a fine sieve to remove cavity's contents and all particles. Add 3 tablespoons mustard to this *fond* and use as sauce.

Ramequins soufflés   Marin
(soufflés baked in a pastry ramequin)

The recipe for the soufflés in these individual pastry ramequins appears to be the ancestor of all soufflés, though Marin
may not have been the inventor. An auxiliary oven capable of
supplying more intense heat than earlier ovens was a recent
invention and made possible the required inflation for a
soufflé, though perhaps not as voluminous an inflation as can
be achieved today. La Varenne referred to the oven as "the
petit four lately come into use in some kitchens."
  The method differed greatly from that used today. Instead
of a roux of butter and flour, choux paste was mixed with an
equal quantity of butter in a mortar and ground with a pestle.
Brie cheese, Gruyère cheese and chopped parsley were then
added, and finally 5 egg yolks. When the pestle had done its
job thoroughly the beaten egg whites were folded in and the
soufflé went into the *petit four*. No part of the soufflé had
been cooked before it went into the oven.
  Baking the soufflé in a pastry container may have been the
invention of the Duc d'Orléans. During his regency he won
acclaim for his *pains d'Orléans*, which may have been soufflés
baked in bread cases or *pains*.
  In individual pastry cases, these make tempting hors-
d'œuvres or an attractive first course for dinner. Choose
round, fluted pastry tins; they come in many sizes, from
bite-size to pie-size. A 3-inch size makes a nice first course.
  Marin's pastry ramequins were made of puff paste. A
cream cheese pastry, given below, is easier to make and
easier to remove from the pastry tins.
  For ten to twelve 3-inch pastry tins: ¾ cup water, 6 tablespoons butter, ½ teaspoon salt, ¾ cup flour, 3 eggs, 3 ounces
soft Brie cheese, and 3 ounces grated Gruyère cheese. For a
sharper cheese taste substitute a stronger cheese for the Brie,
but cheese must be grated or softened.
  Bring the water, butter and salt to a rolling boil. Dump in
the flour all at one time and stir briskly until the mixture
forms a ball and comes away from the sides of the pan. Re-

move from fire. Beat in the eggs, one at a time (do not over-beat), then stir in the cheese. The mixture will be stiff. Lastly, fold in the egg whites, beaten stiff but not dry.

Fill the pastry tins to the rim. Arrange them on a cookie sheet (for easier handling when removing them from the oven) and bake at 375° for 20 minutes, or until nicely puffed. Remove the pastry ramequins from the tins as soon as they are cool enough to handle. Serve hot.

For the cream cheese pastry: Soften ¼ pound butter and ¼ pound cream cheese by mashing with a fork. Combine with 1¼ cups flour and blend until thoroughly mixed. Pat into a flat cake, wrap in wax paper and chill overnight, or for at least eight hours. Roll out thin on a lightly floured board. Cut into rounds a little larger than the tins and fit in, gently pressing the dough into the crimped sides of the tins. Snip off all surplus. It may be re-rolled. No greasing of tins is necessary. The ramequin must be prebaked at 350° for 4 minutes.

Tendrons de veau   Marin
(braised veal riblets)

Madame de Pompadour created many dishes to tempt Louis XV. One such dish, *tendrons d'agneau à la soleil,* is often mentioned in writings about gastronomy, but its preparation is never described. *Tendrons* are riblets cut from the breast of either lamb or veal. Marin, whose recipes reflected the dishes favored at the time of Louis XV, provided several recipes for the preparation of *tendrons.* All of them called for braising in order to make the riblets tender, resulting in a simple but hearty dish. Perhaps this is why the dish pleased Louis. It was certainly a change from pretentious court fare. Madame Pompadour used lamb, but Marin suggested veal, which we also prefer for this dish.

"Cut the veal breast into tendrons the length of your little finger," Marin began his recipe. The butcher will do this for you; they should be pieces about 4 or 5 inches long. Marinate the riblets for at least 1 hour in a mixture of 3 parts vinegar and 1 part oil, to which add some dried or minced fresh basil, minced onion, a few sprigs of parsley, and salt and pepper. Turn the riblets at least once while they marinate. When ready to cook, drain them thoroughly, season lightly with salt, and fry over moderate heat until they are somewhat browned.

Remove the riblets and in the same pan fry a large onion and a large carrot, cut into thin slices. When these vegetables are lightly browned, spoon them into a casserole or roasting pan that can be tightly covered. Place the riblets on top of the vegetables and add ½ to ¾ cup stock or bouillon. Cover and braise in a preheated oven, 325°, for about 1 hour, or until the riblets are tender. Check at intervals, baste occasionally, and add more liquid if needed.

When the riblets are tender, remove from the pan. Spoon out the carrot and onion and mash through a fine sieve. Pour off all fat from the pan and return the vegetable pulp to it. Add enough stock or bouillon to use as a sauce and bring the liquid to a boil. Scrape the sides and bottom of the pan and simmer the liquid for 5 minutes or so. Pour it over the riblets when serving them. Garnish the platter with mounds of string beans and with carrots cut into julienne strips.

This dish cries out for potatoes in some form to accompany it. Potatoes were not yet present on French tables in Marin's time, but modern cooks might serve it with new potatoes, cooked in their skins, then peeled and sprinkled with parsley, or with mashed potatoes prepared in one of the following ways.

Zephyr potatoes

To hot mashed potatoes add salt, white pepper, butter to taste, and enough hot milk to make the mixture very fluffy. Then add ¼ to ½ cup grated sharp cheese and 1 or 2 beaten eggs. Pile the potatoes into a casserole, dot the top with butter, and bake in a preheated oven, 350°, for about 1 hour, or until the top is puffed and brown.

Pains de pomme de terre, frites
(fried potato cakes)

Cook and mash 1 pound Idaho or western potatoes. Add salt to taste and ¼ cup softened butter. Mix thoroughly. Then add ¾ cup flour, and 2 large (or 3 medium) eggs. Again, mix thoroughly. Last add either ¼ cup chopped green scallion tops, or 3 tablespoons chopped chives, or ½ cup grated sharp cheese.

Form the potato mixture into flat cakes about 2½ inches in diameter. Fry gently in a combination of oil and butter, or margarine, until golden brown on both sides.

Navets au blanc à la moutarde   Marin
(turnips in mustard sauce)

Turnips have always enjoyed favor with French cooks. Marin, an imaginative chef, gave the vegetable an unexpected touch, as in this recipe.

Use small white turnips. Scrape them, cut them in thick slices, and cook them in salted water for 35 minutes, or until tender enough to mash. While the turnips cook, prepare 1 cup Béchamel sauce. To it add 3 tablespoons Dijon-type mustard.

Put the turnips through a food mill, or purée in a food processor. Add 4 tablespoons softened butter, 1 medium grated onion, salt and pepper to taste, a few gratings of fresh nutmeg, and ¼ cup of the mustard-Béchamel mixture. Blend thoroughly and put in a baking dish that can go to the table. Cover the turnips with the remaining Béchamel and sprinkle buttered bread crumbs over the top. For this topping, melt 2 or 3 tablespoons butter in a small pan. When the butter sizzles, add ¼ to ½ cup commercial bread crumbs. Stir until the crumbs have absorbed the butter, and add more butter if necessary. Sprinkle them over the top of the turnips. Bake 10 to 15 minutes in a preheated 400° oven. Serve very hot.

Longe de veau en surprise
(stuffed loin of veal)

The French Cook,
Louis Eustache Ude

Have a loin of veal boned. Prepare a stuffing of cooked pork sausage, cooked mushrooms, sautéed minced onion, 2 slices of white bread soaked in milk and squeezed dry, and grind these together on the fine blade of a meat grinder or in a food processor. Season with salt and pepper. Bind the stuffing with rich consommé or thin brown sauce.

Spread the stuffing on the thick side of the loin and roll up. Make sure the ends are tucked in tightly. Skewer the ends and tie the roll in several places to keep it intact. Place in a roasting pan with an onion, some sliced carrots, and a sprig of parsley. Roast uncovered at 300°, allowing 30 minutes per pound. Baste several times during roasting.

Ude's "surprise" touch was added at the end of the roasting period. The meat was brushed with beaten egg yolk, then sprinkled generously with buttered bread crumbs and returned to the oven for another 10 minutes, or until the bread crumbs had adhered thoroughly and browned slightly. Whether or not you add the "surprise," make a sauce using the pan juices and add Madeira or sherry.

Green rice

adapted from Ude

Under *riz aux differentes purées* (rice with various purées) Ude suggested that rice be combined with various herbs and vegetables. When combined with cress, as he suggested, it becomes a lovely green, as it is also when combined with parsley or sorrel. Here is a recipe inspired by Ude's rice:

Melt 2 tablespoons of butter in a casserole. Swirl it around to coat the sides. Combine and pour in 4 cups cooked rice, 2 cups milk, 2 cloves minced garlic, 2 small chopped shallots, 1 cup chopped parsley, a dash of minced dill, chervil, sorrel, or the like, ½ cup grated cheese, and salt and pepper to taste. Bake in a preheated 325° oven for 30 minutes.

Blanquette of fowl marbrée
(ragout of fowl and tongue)

adapted from Ude

Poach a young chicken in a broth containing a clove of garlic and a bay leaf. When tender remove from broth and cool. Have ready a cooked pickled tongue.

Debone the chicken and cut the meat into fair-sized pieces as if for a stew. Allowing a proportion of ⅔ chicken to ⅓ tongue, cut a sufficient quantity of tongue in medium-thick slices, ¼ to ½ inch thick. Trim away all root and divide each slice into 3 to 4 pieces. Combine the chicken and tongue in a casserole.

Use the chicken broth to make a thin velouté. To this add 1 egg yolk thinned with cream, some chopped watercress, and ½ teaspoon sharp horseradish (more if desired, but taste first). Once the egg has been added the sauce must not boil or become overheated. Warm the blanquette on the top of the stove over a very low fire or in the oven at a low heat.

Recipes
from
the Age
of
Carême

Poulets au chutney
(chicken with chutney)

At the beginning of the nineteenth century, France vied with England for power in India. The contest was soon reflected in cookbooks. The restaurateur and noted chef Antoine Beauvilliers was quick to add curried dishes to his *L'Art du Cuisinier* (1814), which covered the standard classics of French cuisine up to that time. Beauvilliers' *poulets kari*, accompanied by rice, inspired a variation that reverses the curry—puts it into the rice and uses a favorite companion of curry on the chicken.

This recipe is for 3 tender young broilers, split in half. Combine ¾ cup oil, 4 tablespoons vinegar, ¾ cup chutney, 1 or 2 garlic cloves, mashed, a few gratings of ginger root, and ½ teaspoon salt. Blend in an electric blender until completely puréed. Season the broiler halves with salt (pepper optional) and place under a preheated broiler, skin side down. Broil under medium heat. When the chicken begins to turn golden, baste with the chutney mixture. The chicken will brown quickly once this starts, so do not begin basting too soon, and watch carefully after it is begun. When nicely browned on the first side, turn and broil in the same manner on the skin side, basting frequently. When browned, transfer to a preheated 325° oven and allow the chicken to cook until it is completely tender. Serve with curried rice.

Riz au kari
(curried rice)

In a heavy skillet melt 3 tablespoons butter. Add 1½ cups raw rice and stir vigorously over moderately low heat until the rice begins to take color and pop. Add 3 cups heated chicken stock (or stock made with bouillon cubes), 1⅛ teaspoons curry, and 1 teaspoon salt. Cover tightly and cook over very low heat until all the liquid is absorbed (20 to 25 minutes). Do not stir, but glance under the lid after 15 minutes to make sure the rice is not too dry. If necessary, add more liquid, but sparingly.

Rice and noodle pilaf

A variation on the previous dish, which adds noodles to the rice.

Put 2 tablespoons butter into a heavy skillet. Add ¼ cup fine uncooked noodles, broken into ½-inch lengths, and cook until they begin to color, stirring all the while. Add 1 cup uncooked rice to the noodles and continue cooking and stirring until the rice begins to color and pop. Add 2½ cups stock (heated) and ¾ teaspoon salt. Cover tightly and cook over low heat until all the liquid is absorbed, about 20 to 25 minutes.

Fanchonettes

adapted from Carême's
Pâtissier Royal Parisien

Grimod de la Reynière made a great to-do about *fanchonettes*, which were created around 1804 by a pâtissier named Rouget who sold them in his pastry shop. He was inspired (said de la Reynière) by the performance of Madame Henri-Belmont in the play *Fanchon*. The *fanchonette* was a small deep tart filled with various flavors of pastry cream and topped with meringue shaped to look like a crown.

Prepare individual tart shells of your favorite pie crust. For an authentic shape, mold them over 3 inch ramequins. Nothing but the depth of the originals will be lost if you use regular tart tins. Bake tarts at 350° for about 10 minutes, or until golden.

When tarts are cold, fill with a pastry cream made with 2 tablespoons flour, ¾ cup milk, 3 tablespoons sugar, 2 egg yolks, pinch of salt, ½ teaspoon vanilla, and 1 tablespoon rum.

Combine the flour with ⅓ of the milk. Stir until smooth. Add the balance of the milk, sugar, and salt and place over a moderate fire. Stir constantly until mixture thickens. Remove from fire and add the beaten egg yolks custard-style by gradually diluting them with the hot mixture and adding them when the mixture has cooled slightly. Return to stove, lower heat, and stir thoroughly but do not boil. Add the vanilla and rum. Cool.

At this point, if you wish to make chocolate *fanchonettes* add 2 squares melted unsweetened chocolate to the cream filling when it has cooled. For mocha, add ½ square melted unsweetened chocolate and ½ teaspoon instant coffee diluted with 1 tablespoon boiling water.

To complete the pastry cream, whip ½ cup heavy cream and fold in. Fill the tart shells ¾ full. Top with meringue made of the 2 egg whites and 5 tablespoons sugar. Brown slightly in a 350° oven for about 3 minutes.

We tried our own *fanchonette* variations with coconut and with almonds. Either of these should be added *before* folding in the whipped cream. Coconut: Fold in ¼ to ½ cup grated fresh coconut. Top meringue with shredded coconut before baking. Almond: Add ¼ to ½ cup grated or crushed toasted almonds. Before baking, top meringue with slivered *untoasted* almonds.

Grande coquille de meringue
(meringue dessert shell)

Meringue surely has a long history in culinary practice, but was not known by that name until the eighteenth century. Perhaps the earliest mention is in Marin's *Les Dons de Comus,* where a recipe is given for little confections called *meringues,* which were split and filled with whipped cream after being baked. Legend has it that a similar confection was invented in 1720 by a Swiss chef working in Mehringhen, a town in Saxe-Coburg-Gotha. It has been assumed that the Swiss named the dainty after the town, but this is a farfetched guess. Recipes did not cross frontiers that quickly in the eighteenth century, nor did Germanic spelling evolve into French so swiftly. In 1739 Marin seemed to be long-familiar with the word *meringue;* he used it four times in his pastry section, and put the beaten egg whites and sugar to other uses as well, for example *œufs en meringues.* Meringue really came into its own in the nineteenth century, when Carême used it in some of his elaborate dishes. Here is a practical and handsome way to use meringue that even Carême would applaud. Though it is *haute cuisine* in appearance, it is a remarkably easy dessert ro prepare.

For a 12-inch shell to serve 6 to 8, you will need 3 large egg whites, ¾ cup sugar, ⅛ teaspoon cream of tartar, ⅛ teaspoon salt, and 1 teaspoon vanilla.

Add the vanilla, salt, and cream of tartar to the egg whites and beat until the whites begin to peak. Continue beating steadily (medium speed if using an electric mixer) while slowly adding ½ cup of the sugar, 1 tablespoon at a time. Beat until the egg whites are quite stiff and the sugar is well absorbed.

Carefully fold in the remaining ¼ cup sugar by hand. Pile the meringue in a well-buttered 12-inch pie or tart dish that can go from oven to table, or use a tin with a removable bottom. Shape the meringue in the form of an empty tart shell. Bake in a preheated oven, 200°, 45 minutes to 1 hour, or until the meringue is quite firm but still white. Under no circumstances should it brown.

Let your imagination roam when filling the shell. Here are a few suggestions:

Fill it with balls of vanilla ice cream and sprinkle blueberries around each ball.

Alternate balls of vanilla ice cream and orange sherbet and dribble orange marmalade over all.

Fill shell with balls of lime sherbet and garnish with fresh raspberries if in season, or with a purée of frozen raspberries.

Arrange handsome strawberries in the shell; touch them lightly with thinned apricot jam, and pipe whipped cream inside the edge of the meringue shell. And so on and on . . .

Make a layer of crushed macaroons in the bottom of the meringue shell. Cover this with vanilla or praline ice cream, slightly softened for easier spreading. Place in the freezer until the ice cream is hard again. To serve, top this with whipped cream and shavings of bitter chocolate made with a vegetable parer. Serve with chocolate or hot fudge sauce.

Whipped cream and meringue have a natural affinity. Here is a sauce that should go well with some of these suggested combinations:

Dessert sauce for meringue shell

Whip ½ pint heavy cream until stiff. Combine the yolk of 1 large egg (or 2 yolks of medium-size eggs) with ¾ cup powdered sugar and beat well. When smooth, combine the egg mixture with the whipped cream. Add 1 teaspoon flavoring—vanilla, rum, or Grand Marnier, for example. Let the sauce chill for several hours before serving.

Another easy way to use meringue dramatically is to bake it

over ice cream. This novel idea was first introduced in Paris, c. 1867, by a Chinese master cook attached to the Chinese mission visiting the city. Soon afterward Dubois presented it in print as *glace au four* (baked ice cream) in his *Cuisine de Tous les Pays.* What with railroads and increased travel, culinary innovations spread faster in the nineteenth century than they had earlier.

At that time cake was not a part of the concoction. Later it was served by Jean Giroix at the Hotel de Paris in Monte Carlo, and called *omelette à la Norvégienne.* Giroix mounted it on cake. In America, mounted on cake, it became baked Alaska. We like to conceal the ice cream in an angel food cake; there, we think, it deserves a special name.

Anneau de glace au four
(ring of ice cream, baked)

A home-baked angel food cake is best, but a commercial cake will do. Cut off the top of the cake at a depth of ½ inch. Carefully remove the inside, leaving a base of ½ to 1 inch and thin walls. Fill the cake with ice cream, slightly softened for easier handling. Replace the top and set the cake in the freezer for several hours to harden the ice cream. Then cover with a meringue made of 4 egg whites, ¼ teaspoon salt, ¼ teaspoon cream of tartar, ½ cup sugar, and ½ teaspoon vanilla.

Add the salt to the egg whites and beat until frothy. Add the cream of tartar and 2 tablespoons sugar and beat until the whites stand in soft peaks. Slowly add the remaining sugar, 1 tablespoon at a time, beating steadily all the while. When the whites stand in stiff peaks add the vanilla.

Cover the cake with the meringue. Swirl a design into the meringue with the tines of a fork or with a knife. Return the meringue-frosted cake to the freezer to wait until you are ready to serve it. At that time have the oven preheated to 450°. Bake the dessert until the meringue begins to brown slightly. This should take no more than 3 to 5 minutes, so watch carefully. Serve with chocolate, or butterscotch sauce, or a fruit sauce of strawberries, raspberries, or canned red cherries, depending on the flavor of the ice cream hidden in the cake.

Beet borscht

Carême was apparently the first to present borscht to French chefs. It was the standard, heavy version—really a potage. This is a meatless borscht to serve cold with a dollop of sour cream.

Cook 2 bunches red (not pink) beets until tender. Grind on the fine blade of a meat grinder or use a food processor. Heat 2 and ½ quarts of water to the boiling point. Return the beets to the water, boil for 5 to 8 minutes. Remove from the fire and add the juice of 1 large or 2 small lemons. Add 1 tablespoon sugar. Cook for a minute. Cool. While the borscht is cooling beat 2 eggs together with 1 tablespoon salt. When the beet broth is cool enough so as not to curdle the eggs, add them custard-style (diluting gradually with a little of the hot liquid) to the beets. Serve cold. Before serving add sour cream to the borscht by stirring it in, custard-style as with the eggs. This will blend it in smoothly. Garnish with sour cream and minced parsley.

Crêpe aux pommes
(apple pancake)

Cuisine de Tous les Pays,
Dubois

Urbain Dubois introduced many foreign dishes to French cooks in this diverse collection of recipes from many countries, and did more than any other French chef to bring an international flavor to French cuisine. The recipes, graced with Dubois's French touch, included many German dishes he had learned to relish during the years he was chef to the king of Prussia. Fortunately for the German recipes, the book was published before the Franco-Prussian war. This pancake may be folded like a French omelette, but is most effective served flat, in the German manner. An attractive brunch or luncheon dish, it will serve one, two, or four persons, depending on what other dishes are served.

Peel and thinly slice 2 cooking apples. Combine ⅓ cup flour, ½ teaspoon salt, ⅛ teaspoon baking powder, and ¼ teaspoon cinnamon, with 1⅛ cups milk, and 3 eggs. Beat with a rotary beater or in an electric mixer until batter is smooth. Add a few drops vanilla extract.

Heat a 10-inch frying pan, preferably one with a rounded bottom and sides. When pan is hot add 4 tablespoons butter and as the butter melts swirl it around and tilt the pan to coat its sides thoroughly. Cover the bottom of the pan with the apples and cook over a medium heat, turning the slices to cook on both sides. When the apples are soft, but not mushy, add enough batter to cover them. Tilt the pan so that the batter will run up and around the sides of the pan. Repeat this almost immediately. When a little more than half the batter has been used in this way (in the course of a few minutes) add the rest of the batter and place the pancake in a preheated oven, 400°.

Bake for 15 to 20 minutes, or until pancake is firm. Carefully remove it from the pan. Sprinkle generously with sugar and cinnamon, and then with powdered sugar.

Caneton aux choucroute
(duckling with sauerkraut)

Cuisine de Tous les Pays,
Dubois

Bake three ducklings. Cut each one into 4 or 6 pieces. Moisten them with a little brown sauce and set aside until time to serve. Meanwhile cook 2 pounds sauerkraut with some small saveloy sausages (highly seasoned pork sausages). Drain the sauerkraut thoroughly. Arrange as a bed for the cut-up ducks. Surround the sauerkraut with the sausages cut into slices.

Carapulca, Spanish fashion   *Cuisine de Tous les Pays,*
                                    Dubois

Cut filet of pork into middling-sized squares. Fry in hot oil along with 12 small onions. When the pork and onions are brown enough, add some smoked ham cut into large dice. Cook the ham with the pork and onions for a few minutes, then add salt, pepper, and a dash of cayenne. Cover with broth and let the stew simmer until the pork is thoroughly tender.

Transfer the stew to an ovenproof casserole. Top with a few fried sausages cut into pieces, and 4 or 5 hard-cooked eggs cut into quarters. Season the eggs with salt and pepper. Sprinkle over the entire casserole some shredded almonds that have been browned in oil and then crushed with a rolling pin. Place the casserole in a moderate oven (325°) for 30 minutes. Serve in the casserole.

Veal aux anchois   *Cuisine de Tous les Pays,*
(veal with anchovies)   Dubois

This is an easy way to perk up a veal roast such as shoulder or round. Make slight gashes in the roast and lard with anchovy filets. Lay a few on top of the roast after first seasoning it. Go lightly on the salt, the anchovies will impart some. Place in a roasting pan with a large sliced onion, a bay leaf, and ½ teaspoon whole allspice. Pour in ¼ cup dry white wine. Roast at 300 or 325°, basting frequently, 2 to 2½ hours, depending on size of roast.

Gnocchi à la romaine   adapted from *La Cuisine Classique,*
                             Dubois and Bernard

In the top of a double boiler heat 4 cups milk, salt and nutmeg to taste. When hot slowly add 1 cup farina, stirring constantly. Cook 3 to 5 minutes (it will thicken quickly; stir as long as you can but it is not necessary to go the full time). Remove from fire, cool slightly and add 3 beaten egg yolks custard-style—that is by diluting them with some of the farina mixture before adding them to the double boiler. Return to heat and stir thoroughly so that yolks are mixed in, but do not overheat. The mixture will be very stiff; it should be.

Butter a large pan, preferably glass. Pour in the farina mixture and pat it down to ½-inch thickness, filling the corners neatly. Smooth top as well as possible. Chill thoroughly. Cut into squares, oblongs, or any shape desired. Place in a well-buttered baking dish, brush with melted butter, and sprinkle with a combination of Gruyère and Parmesan cheese (any cheese that melts nicely will do). Bake at 350° until cheese melts and gnocchi look tempting.

Filets de poulets a la Béarnaise   adapted from *La Cuisine Classique*, Dubois and Bernard

Use large chicken breasts without wings. Skin and bone them and split in half. Allow one half per serving unless breasts are very small. Make an incision at the thick side of the breast and carefully open a space to receive a small amount of stuffing.

For stuffing for *each* breast allow 1 tablespoon finely chopped mushrooms and ½ tablespoon each parsley and tarragon. Sauté the mushrooms briefly in butter, add the herbs, and cook one minute. Spread the mixture on a plate to cool. When cool fill each breast with its share of the stuffing. Press the slit together firmly, using a bit of finely minced raw chicken as a sealer. This should make the edges cook together (one hopes!). If dubious, use toothpicks or small skewers until cooking is completed.

Brush each portion with beaten egg yolk (brushing is a better way to apply egg than dipping—more controlled), then dredge with fine bread crumbs. Shake off all excess.

Heat oil and butter in a skillet that fries dependably. (Iron won't do for this; we use copper or stainless steel.) Fry the breasts over a medium fire for 3 or 4 minutes on each side, or until crisp and brown. Try to serve these piping hot off the fire and take care when first piercing them. They may spurt.

Filets de poulets aux trois fromages
(chicken breasts stuffed with three cheeses)

Here is another way to stuff chicken breasts:
Allow a boneless half-breast per serving. Place the half between two pieces of wax paper and pound with a rolling pin until the meat is quite flat and thin. It should be large enough to wrap around an oblong stick of cheese approximately 3½ inches long, ¾ inches wide, and ½ inch thick.

Several hours in advance of cooking, prepare the cheese filling as follows, adjusting the quantity according to the number of half-breasts to be stuffed. This quantity is for 2 halves: 2 tablespoons softened cream cheese, 2 tablespoons softened Roquefort cheese, and 2 tablespoons Swiss cheese, finely grated.

Mash the cream cheese and Roquefort. Blend together and add the grated Swiss cheese. Mix thoroughly and form into two sticks as described above. It is important that the sticks be thick, so the cheese will not dissipate during cooking. Chill the cheese sticks well; if they are slightly frozen the result will be even better.

When ready to cook, place the cheese on the inner side of the breast (keep the smooth side outside) and wrap as you would a package, the ends carefully tucked in so that the cheese is completely contained. No need to tie the "package"—it will seal during cooking if you start by cooking the side with the overlaps.

Lightly dredge each breast with flour and rub off all surplus. Heat clarified butter, or a mixture of oil and butter (or margarine) in a reliable frying pan. Fry the breasts over moderate heat until golden. Turn to brown on all sides. The entire frying process should not take more than 8 to 10 minutes, perhaps even less, depending on the thickness of the wrapped breast. Serve at once, and take care when making the first stab; the cheese may spurt.

Pommes soufflés (from the Pavillon Henry IV at St. Germain-en-Laye)

This dish, accidentally invented at the Pavillon in 1837 by chef Collinet, is easy to duplicate after a little practice. Slice western or Idaho potatoes into ⅛-inch slices. Cook a few at a time in oil heated to 300°. Remove from the oil and set them aside if you wish to serve them a bit later. If they are to be finished at once, have ready another pan of oil heated to 385°. Drop the potatoes in for their second bath. Remove as soon as they have puffed and browned. Strain thoroughly and set them on paper toweling to absorb all remaining oil. Serve without delay.

Saumon au four, sauce anchois adapted from *La Cuisine Classique*,
(baked salmon with anchovy sauce) Dubois and Bernard

Marinate slices of salmon (¾ to 1 inch thick) for 1 hour in a mixture of oil and vinegar, to which add 1 small crumbled bay leaf and ¼ teaspoon thyme leaves.

Place the salmon slices in a shallow, well-buttered baking dish and bake at 350° for 25 minutes (or until the fish flakes easily). Turn the slices once, midway during the baking period. Baste frequently with butter and lemon juice.

Before attempting to remove the salmon, run a knife under each slice to loosen it. Remove carefully with a pancake turner. Arrange the salmon on a warm serving platter and glaze each slice with butter combined with anchovies pounded to a pulp (or the butter may be mixed with anchovy paste). Let the butter melt on the salmon after it has been combined with the anchovies.

Surround the salmon with small boiled potatoes sprinkled with minced parsley, and decorate the platter with saw-toothed lemon halves.

Recipes from the Age of Escoffier

Volaille à la Derby
(chicken à la Derby)

L'Art Culinaire, 1884
Jean Giroix

This rice-stuffed chicken delighted the Prince of Wales when he visited the Grand Hotel in Monte Carlo in 1883.

Select a tender young chicken weighing about 2½ pounds. Melt 2 tablespoons butter in a heavy skillet. Add ½ cup rice and stir over medium heat until the rice begins to pop. Pour in 1 cup hot bouillon, cover tightly, and cook over a low fire until the rice has absorbed all moisture, about 20 minutes.

Sauté *separately* in butter: 1 minced onion, 1 chicken liver, 3 or 4 large mushrooms, sliced. Chop the liver and mushrooms after sautéing. Fold all three ingredients into the rice, season with salt and pepper, and fill the cavity of the chicken. Close the openings completely, truss the chicken, season it with salt and a dash of white pepper. Apply softened butter to the breast and legs.

Place chicken in a shallow roasting pan (we use ovenproof earthenware) with 1 tablespoon melted butter in the bottom. Add an onion and a carrot, sliced. Place in a preheated oven (450°) for 20 minutes, then reduce temperature to 350°, add ¼ cup white wine, and roast 45 minutes longer or until nicely browned and tender. Baste several times and at each temperature add white wine if needed to prevent scorching.

Remove chicken, carrots, and onion from pan. Skim off as much fat as possible. Add ¼ cup brandy to the pan and reheat. Add stock or bouillon to make sufficient sauce to serve over chicken, bring to boiling point and cook for 1 minute, stirring constantly.

(Giroix first browned the chicken in a skillet. Oven browning is easier. He garnished the serving dish with slices of foie gras, lightly floured and sautéed in butter. Nice if you have it on hand.)

Poulet sauté à la Grenobloise   *L'Art Culinaire*, 1885
(chicken in the style of Grenoble)

This recipe is signed "E." Since there was no other "E" among the founding contributors to *L'Art Culinaire,* this must be Escoffier. It has his voice. It is presented exactly as he wrote it.

Cut up a tender young chicken. Season it well and sauté it in butter until it is nicely browned. Pour on a glass [¼ cup] of good cognac, cover and let cook over a low fire for 30 minutes. When tender remove the chicken and keep it warm while you chop up a shallot and a clove of garlic. Cook these together in butter along with a sprig of tarragon. Add this to the pan juices in which the chicken cooked. Strain the juices and pour over the chicken. Serve.

(Escoffier was very partial to sauces based on the pan juices. However, before adding anything to the pan he would first have poured off all fat. Then he would have added the shallot, garlic, and tarragon and some stock. This would have been swirled around and cooked down so as to acquire the flavor of the added ingredients. It was not necessary to tell an experienced chef, reading *L'Art Culinaire*, anything so obvious.)

Filets de truites au lac Vert   *L'Art Culinaire*, 1885
                                                   Niquet

For this dish use trout filets. Prepare 2 cups fish broth from scraps of fish, or use clam juice diluted with water. To this add shallots, onion, garlic, thyme, parsley, and 1 cup white wine. Cook gently for about 15 minutes, then strain.

Prepare a roux of 2 tablespoons butter and 1 tablespoon

L'Art de bien faire les Glacés

flour (slightly less if you use cornstarch instead of flour; it will make a smoother sauce). Add the fish broth to the roux and blend until smooth, then add ¼ cup cream.

Place the fish filets in a buttered shallow gratin dish. Cover with half the sauce and bake in a preheated oven (350°) for 20 to 25 minutes. When the fish tests nearly done, add the remaining sauce, to which chopped parsley and chopped tarragon or chervil (or any combination of two green herbs) have been added. Bake a few minutes longer.

Aubergines sautées à la Provençal   L'Art Culinaire, 1888
(sautéed eggplant Provencal)   P.C. Dessoliers

Dessoliers had been *chef de cuisine* at the court of Sweden. He was among the earliest contributors to *L'Art Culinaire*.

Slice an eggplant into 1-inch-thick slices. Sprinkle with salt and let stand 30 minutes. Press out all moisture and cut eggplant slices into cubes. Dredge lightly with flour and shake off all excess.

In heated oil sauté 2 large minced onions. As onion begins to grow glassy, add cubed eggplant and continue cooking until both vegetables are tender and slightly browned. Season with salt and pepper. Garnish with chopped parsley.

Pommes Maire   L'Art Culinaire, 1885
(potatoes in cream)

Prosper Salles, who along with Prosper Montagné wrote *La Grande Cuisine Illustrée* (1900), contributed this recipe but did not originate it. It was a specialty of the Restaurant Maire, where Escoffier was *chef de cuisine* in 1884. *L'Art Culinaire* commented, "This restaurant is one of the finest in Paris and it must have merited the fine reputation. It is good to add that the incontestable talent of its administration and chefs has contributed to placing this restaurant in the first rank."

New potatoes are boiled in their skins in salted water for 20 minutes, then peeled, sliced, covered with milk, dotted with butter, seasoned, and set in a moderate oven to bake until the milk is absorbed and the potatoes are thoroughly soft. Just before serving, thick cream is poured over the potatoes and the dish is returned to the oven for another 10 minutes, until the cream is somewhat absorbed. The potatoes are then run under the broiler for a few minutes to give them a delicate tinge.

Gigot en chamois, sauce Mauresque   *L'Art Culinaire*, 1885
(marinated leg of lamb)   Thomas Genin

Thomas Genin was a founder of the Société Culinaire Française, sponsors of *L'Art Culinaire*.

Select a young leg of lamb. Prepare a marinade of equal parts red wine and vinegar. Add salt, 2 bay leaves, ½ teaspoon thyme, and 7 cloves of garlic, one of them crushed. Place the lamb in a suitable dish, pour the marinade over it, and cover tightly with a napkin or towel. Marinate the lamb for 24 hours, turning it once or twice.

Preheat oven to 400°. Roast lamb 20 minutes, then reduce temperature to 325°. Continue roasting, allowing 15 minutes per pound for medium-rare lamb.

For the sauce, reduce ½ cup marinade and ½ cup brown stock or consommé slightly thickened. Add 1 teaspoon butter. At this point we part company with Genin, who adds ½ cup chicken blood. We add a scant ¼ cup of red wine and throw a tablespoon of capers into the sauce.

A similar recipe for leg of lamb appeared soon after Genin's, *Gigot de Behague*. It bears out the theory (see Chapter 14) that lamb *de Behague*, frequently prepared by Escoffier at the Moulin Rouge in Paris, meant lamb raised in the pastures of the Count de Behague. Escoffier's dish was *selle d'agneau de Behague* (saddle of lamb). The saddle may be treated in the same way as the leg in the following recipe. Escoffier served his lamb with a garlic-tomato sauce. This recipe produces its own sauce.

Gigot à la eau-de-vie

adapted from a nineteenth-century recipe,

(marinated leg of lamb with brandy)

chef unknown

Trim off all surplus fat from a leg of lamb, leaving only a very thin layer to protect exposed flesh. Marinate the leg in red wine, to which add 1 large carrot, 1 large minced or sliced onion, 1 bay leaf, ⅛ teaspoon thyme leaves, 6 cloves garlic, 6 minced shallots, a few grinds of whole black pepper, and 6 juniper berries (or substitute 2 tablespoons gin for the juniper berries). Marinate for at least 12 hours, longer if possible.

To cook, season the lamb with salt and pepper. Place it in a roasting pan and sprinkle a few leaves of thyme over it—just a suspicion of thyme will do. Roast at 350°, allowing 10 to 12 minutes per pound for rare to medium, 15 minutes per pound for well done. (A roasting thermometer is recommended for best results, as ovens can differ greatly.) Baste frequently with the marinade. When lamb is done, remove it from the roasting pan and skim off all fat from the drippings. Return the lamb to the pan and pour over it ⅓ cup brandy.

Again remove lamb from pan and keep it warm until ready to serve. Add enough stock to the brandy in the pan to make the desired quantity of sauce. Cook for a few minutes and scrape the bottom and sides of the pan as the sauce cooks. Strain before serving, if necessary.

Haricots blancs (white beans) would be an appropriate French touch with either of these lamb dishes.

Haricots blancs à la Parmesan
(white beans in Béchamel sauce with Parmesan cheese)

For this dish use the white beans commonly called navy beans. Soak 2 cups beans for 2 hours in enough water to cover them. (It is not necessary to soak them overnight.) After soaking pour off the water and put the beans in a pot with a tight-fitting cover. Add to them 4 cups water, 1 medium whole carrot, 1 medium onion stuck with 1 clove, a few sprigs of parsley, and ½ teaspoon salt. Cover, bring to the boil, and simmer gently for 2½ to 3 hours, or until the beans are tender but firm. Add water during cooking if necessary.

When properly tender, drain the beans and transfer them to a casserole.

Prepare a Béchamel sauce of 1½ tablespoons butter, 1½ tablespoons flour or cornstarch, 1½ cups milk, and ¼ cup cream added at the last. Have ready ⅓ to ½ cup grated Parmesan cheese. Add salt and pepper to taste to the beans and fold in the grated cheese. Then add the Béchamel sauce. Place in a preheated oven, 350°, and bake for 15 to 20 minutes. Serve very hot.

Poulet à la Castenette
L'Art Culinaire, 1885
(no chef given)

Quarter a tender young chicken. Sauté it in butter mixed with oil and a clove of mashed garlic. When the chicken attains a nice color transfer it to a casserole and place it on a thinly sliced Spanish onion. Place around the chicken 2 or 3 medium-size tomatoes, peeled, seeded, and quartered; julienne strips of strongly flavored ham such as Bayonne or Smithfield, and a bouquet garni. Add salt, pepper, and ⅓ cup Madeira. Cover loosely and finish the cooking in a preheated oven (350°), 30 to 40 minutes. Arrange the chicken on a platter, garnish with toast rounds covered with small thick scallops of ham sautéed in butter.

Sauces d'Autriche
(Austrian sauces)

L'Art Culinaire, 1890
Alfred Cecchi

Cecchi, an early *collaborateur* of *L'Art Culinaire*, was apparently employed in Austria. He found these sauces new and interesting at the time and introduced them to his colleagues.

Horseradish sauce with almonds

Prepare 1 cup of Béchamel sauce (or less, depending on what quantity is wanted). To it add cream equaling ⅓ of its volume (to 1 cup sauce, ⅓ cup cream). Then add ⅓ cup grated almonds, 5 or 6 tablespoons grated horseradish, a pinch of cayenne pepper, and a pinch of sugar. Blend together.

Currant-horseradish sauce

Melt 8 ounces of currant jelly. Add 1 tablespoon sharp mustard and 4 tablespoons grated horseradish. Blend together.

Horseradish apple sauce

For this excellent accompaniment to pot roast, unsugared apple sauce made of red apples cooked in their skins will produce a tempting pink sauce. Combine 1 cup of sauce with ¼ cup grated horseradish and 1 tablespoon sugar.

All these sauces should be served chilled.

Truite à l'aïoli
(trout with garlic sauce)

L'Art Culinaire, 1890
G. Garlin

Whole trout are cooked in an open pot on top of the stove, as if for bouillabaisse.

Sauté a large onion (thinly sliced) and 2 cloves of garlic in hot oil until glassy. Transfer to a cooking pot. Add a shredded carrot, a bay leaf, and the trout. Pour on enough liquid (½ white wine, ½ fish broth or water) to cover the number of trout to be cooked. Heat almost to the boiling point, reduce heat, and simmer for about 15 minutes or until trout flakes easily at the touch of a fork. Remove and keep warm while a few scallops and mussels are poached in the broth to serve as garnish for the trout. Serve with *aïoli* sauce.

Aïoli sauce: Mash 3 large cloves of garlic to a fine pulp. Combine with a raw egg yolk. Add 1 cup olive oil slowly, stirring constantly until mixture resembles a thick mayonnaise.

The trout may be served cold. In this case eliminate the scallops and mussels and garnish the fish with marinated cucumber slices and/or small canned shrimp, also marinated.

Bœuf Strogonoff	*L'Art Culinaire,* 1891
[sic]	Charles Brière

This is an early, if not the first, mention of this popular dish. At the time Brière was employed in St. Petersburg, Russia.

Cut the ends of a beef tenderloin into pieces as if for a goulash. Sauté them quickly over a medium fire. Have ready a sauce made as follows: a large onion, minced and sautéed in butter to which is added 2 tablespoons tomato purée, 1 tablespoon *Sauce Espagnole* or brown stock, and 4 tablespoons sour cream. Combine this with the beef and heat, but avoid making it too hot lest the cream curdle. Serve in a tureen with *pommes sautées.*

Brière's suggestion of crisp potatoes does seem a better choice, and a better contrast, than the usual cooked noodles or rice.

Alose grillée à l'oiselle   *L'Art Culinaire*, 1894
(shad with sorrel)

Take a whole shad or large filets and brush with oil on both sides. Season with salt and pepper, arrange in a shallow baking dish, dot liberally with butter, and place in a preheated oven (400°). Bake 15 minutes, reduce heat to 350°, and bake another 15 minutes. Baste fish with butter and lemon juice several times during baking. Filets should be ready at the end of 30 minutes. A whole fish will take longer, perhaps 45 minutes. It is done when the flesh flakes easily at the touch of a fork.

While the fish bakes, cook and purée the sorrel. Season with salt, pepper, and butter. Remove fish from oven a few minutes before it is done; top it with the sorrel and return to the oven to finish baking.

Spinach may be used instead of sorrel and will be improved with the addition of 2 tablespoons lemon juice. It should be thoroughly free of moisture before the lemon juice is added.

Bananes frites   *L'Art Culinaire*, 1894
                    Ernest Glass

Ernest Glass was employed by an American millionaire and moved with the family between New York City and the family's summer home in Beverly, Massachusetts, sending recipes from both places. He urged French chefs to become acquainted with bananas.

"Americans love this fruit," he wrote his colleagues. I've used them in fruit *entremets* with good results. I believe my colleagues in France will want to do the same. After all, it is only a substitution of one fruit for another; the base of these *entremets* is French and classic."

Glace aux bananes was banana ice cream. *Omelette aux bananes* was made with 6 eggs and 2 or 3 small bananas, sliced. Just before serving the *omelette,* Glass finished it off with a dash of rum.

Bananes frites are particularly good served as a side dish with fowl or veal. For this use large firm bananas cut in half and then split into quarters. Brush each piece with beaten egg, sprinkle lightly with a mixture of nutmeg, sugar, and cinnamon, then roll in fine bread crumbs. Sauté gently over moderate heat in butter and oil until golden on all sides.

Bananas flambée

Bananas make a dramatic as well as delicious desert when prepared in a flat crêpe pan on a chafing dish stand, with the entire procedure taking place at the dining room table. If you lack a chafing dish, prepare the bananas in an ordinary skillet in the kitchen, then transfer them to a serving dish and bring them into the dining room to set aflame. They will be best if prepared just before serving.

Have ready 5 very firm medium-size bananas, slightly underripe. Split them lengthwise and sprinkle the rounded side of each half with cinnamon.

In the cooking pan melt 6 tablespoons butter, add 4 table-spoons light brown sugar, and stir constantly, over low heat, until sugar is dissolved. And ¼ cup rum and/or cointreau. When the mixture begins to bubble add the bananas, cut side down. Turn them carefully several times as they cook, to coat them thoroughly with the syrup. They should cook about 5 minutes or less.

When ready to serve, add ¼ cup brandy, warmed beforehand. To make certain that the dessert flames properly, try a specially formulated flambé mix, which is available in most stores that specialize in fine foods. The bananas will be just as delicious if not set aflame.

For a variation, add a scoop of vanilla ice cream to each serving. And for another variation, prepare the syrup as above, but instead of adding rum to the butter-sugar mixture, add 2 tablespoons strong black coffee, 2 tablespoons orange juice, and 2 tablespoons Grand Marnier or kirsch. Before setting the bananas aflame, sprinkle them with cooked shreds of orange rind and slivered almonds.

Hachis de dindon *L'Art Culinaire, 1894*
(Brown turkey hash) Ernest Glass

Combine ground cooked turkey with an equal proportion of ground cooked potatoes. Season with salt and pepper. Add enough rich consommé to moisten and bind while it bakes, "and some chopped onion cooked in butter if it is to be to the taste of the amphitryon." Bake in the form of a large pancake until brown on both sides. (Bake at 350° in a heavy skillet until brown on the bottom. If not brown enough on top, run under the broiler for a few minutes.)

Noisettes d'agneau *L'Art Culinaire, 1894*
(in various styles and prepared
by Escoffier in various places)

Noisettes are the meaty centers of rib and loin chops in lamb and veal, removed from the bone and trimmed of all fat. They are usually sautéed, sometimes placed on a platform of toast, and garnished in various ways. Serving only the centers of these expensive chops is very *grande cuisine* and rather extravagant. But it is an elegant way to serve them. For less elegant occasions, the garnishes will make effective accompaniments for the chops left whole. The recipes are presented as Escoffier gave them to readers of *L'Art Culinaire*. They should offer ample inspiration for those who like to experiment.

Noisettes Moscovite, Moulin Rouge, 1875

The noisette is placed atop a pastry shell that has been filled with macaroni combined with julienned truffles, Parmesan cheese, and cream sauce.

Noisettes d'agneau Cendrillon, Moulin Rouge, 1875

The noisette is placed atop an artichoke fond that has been filled with onion purée in cream sauce—actually a thick soubise sauce—sprinkled with Parmesan cheese, and browned quickly under the broiler before the noisette is placed on the artichoke.

Noisettes d'agneau Georgette, Hotel National, Lucerne, 1886

The noisette is placed on toast, then topped with a small chicken croquette and moistened with *glace de viande.* It is escorted by a mound of potatoes cut in rounds and sautéed to crisp perfection.

Noisettes à la Dûbarry, Grand Hotel, Monte Carlo, 1887

This is one of the simplest presentations. The noisette is placed on a toast round and covered with a *sauce chasseur.* For this cook sliced mushrooms and finely chopped shallots in butter until soft. Add white wine, cognac, a dash of cayenne pepper, chopped parsley or tarragon, and some *Sauce Espagnole.* At the moment of serving pour over the noisettes.

Noisettes Sans-Gêne, Savoy Hotel, London

These were dedicated to Réjane, "the charming interpreter of Madame Sans-Gêne." Butter small individual molds for *pommes Anna* (custard cups will do nicely). Instead of toast, the potatoes serve as the base for the noisette. For the potatoes: slice raw potatoes into thin rounds. Arrange them in the buttered molds, taking care to line the sides of the molds first, then fill the centers, layering the potatoes. Sprinkle each layer lightly with salt and dot with butter. Place in a 450° oven and bake 30 to 35 minutes, or until nicely browned.

Unmold the potatoes and top each mound with a noisette. In the center of the platter make a heap of quartered artichoke *fonds* sautéed in butter. Top each noisette with some *glace viande* thinned with lemon juice and melted butter. Sprinkle *fines herbes* (parsley, chives, and tarragon) over each noisette.

Poulet reine à l Echenard

Poulet reine à lEchenard   *L'Art Culinaire*, 1895

A chef's name was not given but Escoffier was probably responsible for the recipe. At this time Echenard was manager of the Savoy Hotel under Ritz and Escoffier.

Season a young chicken with salt and a liberal sprinkling of paprika and place in an earthenware casserole with a clove of garlic, a *bouquet garni*, and 6 or 8 artichoke bottoms blanched in boiling water and rubbed with lemon juice. Cover the casserole tightly, place in a preheated oven (375°), and bake until chicken is golden, about 45 minutes. Check for tenderness at that time. If chicken is sufficiently cooked, remove the garlic and all fat that has accumulated.

Pour ¼ cup cognac over the chicken. Have ready several tomatoes, peeled, seeded and quartered, that have been lightly sautéed in oil and butter. Add these to the chicken and artichokes.

Fonds d'artichauts à la Genoise   *L'Art Culinaire*, 1898
(artichoke bottoms with spinach)   V. Marchand

Marchand, who presented this as a previously unpublished recipe and therefore new to fellow chefs (and possibly originated by him), became a contributor to *L'Art Culinaire* in 1894.

Cut off top half of artichokes and remove all outside short leaves. Cut off stems flush with the bottoms and rub this cut part with lemon juice to check discoloration. Place artichokes in a roomy saucepan, cover with boiling water, add salt and 2 tablespoons vinegar. Cover and cook over medium heat for 30 to 35 minutes, or until artichokes are tender. Drain thoroughly, remove all remaining leaves, and carefully take out choke.

For 6 or 8 artichoke bottoms prepare ¾ cup cooked chopped spinach. In olive oil sauté 2 tablespoons minced onion and a whole garlic clove. When onion is soft and turning color, remove garlic. Add 1 tablespoon flour, salt, pepper, the cooked spinach, 2 or 3 anchovy filets, minced, and some slightly thickened bouillon to moisten and bind. Pile this mixture into the hollows of the artichoke bottoms. Sprinkle with bread crumbs that have been stirred in melted butter, dot with additional butter, and bake at 350° for about 10 minutes or until crumbs are nicely crusted.

Soles aux aubergines
L'Art Culinaire, 1898
Escoffier

Allow a nice thick filet of sole for each serving. Dip each filet in milk, season with salt and pepper, then dredge lightly with flour, rub off all excess flour, and cook in a frying pan as for *à la meunière*. Have ready 2 or 3 eggplants cut into medium-thick slices. Dip each slice in flour, shake off all excess and sauté in olive oil and butter until nicely browned. Arrange the sole and the eggplant alternately on a warm platter. Sprinkle with lemon juice and chopped parsley and pour on some browned butter, which should be bubbling hot as it reaches the platter. Serve promptly.

Pommes Mirette
L'Art Culinaire, 1898
freely adapted from a recipe by Escoffier

Slice 4 medium-large potatoes into thin slices. Cook them in boiling salted water until tender and almost ready to eat. Rinse them in cold water to make handling easier.

Cut 6 or 8 large mushrooms into julienne strips and sauté

in butter until soft. Arrange the mushrooms and potatoes neatly in a buttered casserole. Season with salt and white pepper. Pour on 2 or 3 tablespoons well-seasoned bouillon or consommé thickened slightly with cornstarch—only enough for the potatoes to absorb in 10 minutes in the oven. Sprinkle shredded Gruyère cheese mixed with grated Parmesan over the top of the casserole. Dot with butter and place in a medium-hot oven (400°) for 8 to 10 minutes, or until the cheese begins to melt and the consommé is absorbed.

Mère Thérèse's   from Escoffier's notes
Gigot d'agneau au sauge
(leg of lamb with sage)

Make gashes in the fatty part of a young leg of lamb and insert sage in each gash. Season the lamb with salt and freshly ground black pepper (and garlic, if you like). Place the lamb in a shallow roasting pan. Surround it with small onions, potatoes, and Jerusalem artichokes (potatoes and artichokes should be parboiled for 5 minutes). Place in a preheated oven (450°) for 15 minutes. Reduce heat to 350° and allow 15 minutes per pound for medium-rare lamb. Roast uncovered; baste meat and vegetables a few times with the pan juices.

Les Foies de Canards   from Escoffier's notes
à la Mère Thérèse
(sautéed duck livers)

Cut duck livers (or large chicken livers) into fairly thick slices, half an inch or more. Season them with salt and pepper and dredge lightly with flour. Rub off all the flour. Dip the slices into beaten egg and then into very fine bread crumbs. Shake off all excess. Sauté gently in clarified butter or a combination of butter and oil, no more than two minutes on each side. Don't overcook. Escoffier called these a *véritable délice*.

Poires Bohémienne   from Escoffier's notes

Choose solid pears of medium size suitable for cooking. Peel them, leaving them whole, and cook gently in a syrup of 2 cups water and ¾ cup sugar until they are tender. Cool them in their syrup.

For 6 to 8 pears melt 5 ounces of apricot marmalade and add enough of the cooking syrup to obtain a slightly thick purée. Add ⅓ cup rum to the purée.

Cover the bottom of a bowl with vanilla ice cream. (Escoffier specified a crystal bowl.) Drain the pears and arrange them in a circle on top of the ice cream. In the center make a mound of *marrons glacés* (or use fresh strawberries, fresh pineapple, or whatever fruit is available and complementary to the pears). Pour the apricot purée over the pears and whatever you have chosen for the center.

Crevettes pimentées   inspired by Escoffier's notes
(spicy shrimps)

Recipes for cooking shrimps (*crevettes*) or crayfish (*langoustines*) were almost nonexistent in French cookbooks until early in the twentieth century. Not that shellfish were absent from French kitchens, especially those practicing *haute cuisine*, but shrimps and the like were mostly used for garnishes, bisques, and shellfish butters to be added to sauces for fish. Escoffier presented a few shellfish recipes in the *Guide* (1902), but the following original recipe was inspired by one in his notes.

Peel and devein 1 pound shrimps. Dredge lightly with flour and shake off all surplus flour. Then brush each shrimp lightly with beaten egg to which salt has been added.

Into a sauté pan large enough to hold the shrimps comfortably, pour enough cooking oil to cover the bottom—at least ¼ inch. Slice a large onion into the oil, add ¼ teaspoon thyme leaves, 1 crushed bay leaf, and 1 or 2 small red chili peppers, crushed. Heat the oil slowly over moderate heat and stir it as it heats so that it will be permeated by the flavor of the spices. Test the flavor on a bit of bread before adding the shrimps. Do not let the oil reach a smoking temperature, but keep it hot enough to cook the shrimps quickly. Depending on the size of the shrimps, this should take from 5 to 8 minutes. Have ready a few tablespoons of julienne strips of ham, sautéed in butter. Garnish the shrimps with the ham and serve with watercress sauce.

Sauce de cresson
(watercress sauce)

Pick over ½ bunch watercress, remove all but one inch of the stems, and blanch the cress in boiling water for a few seconds. Dry thoroughly. Chop the cress coarsely. Mash 1 hard-cooked egg with a fork. Combine the cress, egg, and 1 medium onion, chopped fine, in a blender, along with ¼ cup mayonnaise. If the blender requires additional liquid to operate, add a little bit of cream. When thoroughly combined and puréed in the blender, remove to a mixing bowl and add ¾ cup more mayonnaise. Add salt to taste, and the merest dash of white pepper.

Soupe de cresson

Though watercress is popular in French cookery today, and was known and relished in antiquity, it received little attention in French cuisine until the nineteenth century. It is as well entrenched as sorrel now, and much easier to obtain in American markets. Therefore it seems fitting to include a recipe for the delicious soup it makes.

Wash 1 bunch watercress. Leave a small portion of stem on each plant. Pour boiling water over the cress and let stand for 1 minute. Strain and chop coarsely.

Melt 3 tablespoons butter in a 3-quart saucepan. In it sauté 1 medium sliced onion and 3 sliced scallion ends (white part) until transparent. Do not brown. Add 2 cups sliced Idaho or western potatoes, 2 cups boiling water, and 1 teaspoon salt. Reduce heat and cook, covered, until the potatoes are soft. Add 2½ cups chicken stock, 1 cup milk, and the chopped watercress. Bring again to the boil, reduce heat, cover, and simmer for 10 minutes. Purée in a blender, 1 cup at a time.

Return to saucepan and add ½ cup cream. Serve hot, garnished with watercress leaves. If soup is too thick (a matter of personal taste), thin it with additional stock or use dissolved chicken bouillon cubes.

Guinea hen à la châtelaine   from Escoffier's notes

This stuffing recipe is for 5 guinea hens, 10 servings of ½ hen per person. It will be equally suitable for Cornish hens or squab chickens.

To 1 pound minced cooked pork sausage add ½ cup chopped mushrooms sautéed in butter, ½ cup fresh bread crumbs tossed in butter, and 2 medium onions, minced. Blend these ingredients together and moisten with some white stock and 1 or 2 tablespoons brandy.

Stuff the birds and tie or truss them securely so that they can be browned in a skillet before going into the oven. When browned, roast them at 375° for 45 to 60 minutes. Cover them for part of the time to avoid having them dry out. When they are tender, remove the birds from the roasting pan and pour off all fat. (In our kitchen, after the fat is poured off from a roasting pan, paper toweling is used to blot up whatever fat remains. Then we proceed with making the sauce in the pan.)

After removing the fat, add 1 cup white wine to the pan and scrape the bottom and sides. Cook over low heat on top of the stove until liquid is somewhat reduced. Strain it if cooking particles are apparent. Before serving, add 1 cup thinned sour cream or sour half-and-half.

To serve, separate the birds into two halves. Divide the stuffing into equal mounds on a serving platter and place a bird half on top of each mound. Garnish with fried parsley.

Persil frite
(fried parsley)

Preparing this elegant garnish is almost as easy as boiling water. Use fresh, crisp parsley. Separate it into flowerlets leaving 1-inch stems. Wash in cold water, drain thoroughly, and wrap loosely in toweling to insure that all moisture is removed, or spread the parsley out to dry.

Place the parsley in a frying basket or flat-bottomed sieve. Do not crowd it. If possible, keep it in a single layer. Immerse the parsley in hot (but not smoking) oil. Remove it the minute it is crisp and let it drain on paper toweling. The frying may take from seconds to a minute or so.

In the home of Swiss industrialist Robert von Hirsch, noted art collector and host, fried parsley was frequently served before dinner as an hors-d'œuvre, along with apéritifs.

Potage au potiron
(pumpkin soup)

adapted from
the *New Century Cookery Book*
Herman Senn

Saute ½ small onion, minced, in 2 tablespoons butter. In a saucepan, over low heat, combine the onion with 1½ cups canned or cooked mashed pumpkin. Have ready 2 slices stale bread, crusts removed, soaked in milk for 10 minutes. Squeeze out the milk and mash the bread with a fork. Add to it a pinch of sugar and nutmeg, and salt and pepper to taste, then blend into the pumpkin. Slowly add 4 cups chicken stock and 2 cups milk, both previously warmed. Add a bay leaf and cook the soup for about 20 minutes over low heat, stirring occasionally. Skim if necessary. Watch carefully to avoid scorching the soup. At the end of the cooking time remove the bay leaf and let the soup cool slightly. Dilute 2 beaten egg yolks with a little of the soup, then slowly and gradually add them to it. Finally, stir in ¼ cup of cream.

If necessary to reheat the soup, do so over low heat and do not allow it to boil or the cream and eggs will curdle. Serve garnished with fried bread croutons.

Frozen mousse   adapted from a recipe by Herman Senn
à la Pückler-Muskau

Soak 1 tablespoon unflavored gelatin in 3 tablespoons cold
water. Combine 1 cup puréed apricots or peaches, ½ cup
sugar, and the grated rind and juice of 1 lemon. Stir in the
softened gelatin and stir over cracked ice until mixture begins
to thicken, or place in refrigerator until thick and syrupy.
Fold in 2 tablespoons Curaçao and 1 cup heavy cream, stiffly
whipped, and turn into a pan that will fit in the freezer. For a
smoother mousse, stir again before it is thoroughly frozen.

Heap into individual serving dishes and garnish with
crushed macaroons. Return them to the freezer until time to
serve dessert.

A few notes on sauces

It is helpful to know how to go about creating stock for
sauces, even though in many cases a creditable sauce can be
made from pan juices alone when wine, liquor, mushroom
essence, or other such touches are added. Bouillon or consommé is also very helpful and may be used full strength if a
strong stock is wanted. However it is made, a clear sauce de-
void of any hint of fat is the ideal. Thorough chilling of the
stock, or of the pan sauce after it is made, will bring every
speck of fat to the surface.

Basic brown stock

Use 1 pound chuck, plate, or soup meat, or 2 pounds beef
short ribs, and 3 pounds veal knuckle and veal bones (have
the bones cracked). Place the meat, along with 2 large carrots,
cut up, 1 large sliced onion, 3 shallots, and 2 large stalks of
celery, cut up, in a roasting pan in a hot (450°) oven and roast
uncovered for about 20 minutes. Reduce heat to 375° and
continue roasting for another 30 minutes. Check often to see
that nothing burns and to turn meat and vegetables so that
everything browns nicely. When browning is completed,
transfer the contents of the roaster to a large soup kettle. Pour
off all fat. Pour 1 or 2 cups boiling water into the roasting pan.

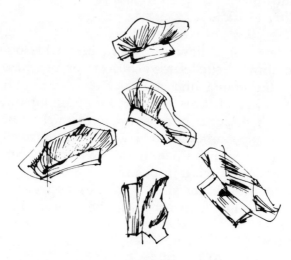

Loosen all scraps that cling to the pan and cook on top of the stove for a few minutes, continuing to stir and loosen all residue. Pour this into the soup pot along with 10-12 cups of water. Add 1 bay leaf, ¼ teaspoon allspice (optional), a few sprigs of parsley, salt, and a dash of white pepper. Bring to the boiling point and immediately reduce to simmer. Cover and simmer for 3 hours. Skim at frequent intervals.

At end of cooking add 1 tablespoon soy sauce. Remove bones and meat and strain carefully. Set aside to cool; then chill. When fat rises to the top, skim off every trace.

White stock

White stock is made the same way as brown stock, using chicken backs, necks, and wings instead of beef, but including veal. If veal is not included it is a chicken stock, but even for this a few cracked veal bones are desirable for their gelatinous contribution.

The basic white sauces

These sauces all begin with a roux of 4 tablespoons of butter and 4 tablespoons of flour (slightly less of cornstarch or arrowroot, which is what Escoffier used instead of flour and many fine chefs follow his lead). To this add 2 cups of liquid. This proportion produces a medium-thick sauce. It may be made thicker or thinner by increasing or lessening the butter and starch. Salt and pepper to taste are added to all sauces. The liquid added is what mainly differentiates the sauces.

If the liquid added is milk, the white sauce becomes *Béchamel*, the most basic of the white sauces. Part of the liquid may be cream for a richer *Béchamel*. (Some authorities add chicken stock to a *Béchamel* but this is merely confusing.)

If the liquid added is chicken, veal, or fish stock, the sauce becomes a *Velouté*.

If cream is added to the *Velouté* it becomes *Sauce Suprême*.

If 2 large egg yolks and 2 teaspoons of lemon juice are added to the *Sauce Suprême* it becomes *Sauce Allemande*. (*L'Art Culinaire* failed to get the name changed.)

Basic brown sauce

In the brown sauce family the equivalent of basic *Béchamel* is *Sauce Espagnole*. It begins with a roux of 2 tablespoons of butter (or beef, veal, or pork drippings) and 2 tablespoons starch. The starch should be allowed to brown somewhat, but take care that it does not burn. Stir and cook the fat and starch until it is toast colored, then add 2 cups basic brown stock and 1 tablespoon tomato paste or 2 tablespoons thick tomato purée. A bay leaf and a pinch of thyme is then added and the sauce is set to simmer over very low heat for at least 30 minutes.

If brown stock is not on hand, consommé may be used instead, and will probably work best if it is not fully diluted.

Almost anything that enters the cook's mind may be added to basic sauces and may result in something that already has a name in the wide lexicon of sauces. Ude added the juice of parsley and spinach to *Sauce Allemande,* for example, and called it "green Hollandaise."

Glace de viande

This is brown stock, cooked down until it is syrupy and thick enough to coat the back of a spoon. The stock should be cooked down to half its volume, then strained through several thicknesses of cheesecloth to remove all sediment. This process of cooking down and straining should be repeated several times until the rich, thick *glace* is obtained. Finish it by adding a spoonful of Madeira or mushroom essence.

Bibliography

Anquetil, Louis Pierre. *Memoirs of the Court of France.* Edinburgh: Bell & Bradfute, 1791.

Argenson, René Louis de Voyer de Palmy. *Journal et Memoires.* Paris: 1859.

Allemand, Maurice (pseud. Maurice Allem). *La Vie Quotidienne sous le Deuxième Empire.* Paris: Hachette, 1948.

Barbier, Edmond Jean François. *Chronique de la Régence et du Règne du Louis XV, or Journal de Barbier.* Paris: Charpentier, 1858.

Berry, Mary. *Social Life in England and France.* London: Richard Bentley, 1844.

Brogan, Denis W. *Development of Modern France.* London: Hamilton, 1940.

Cobban, Alfred. *A History of Modern France.* New York: Braziller, 1965.

Desnoiresterres, Gustav Le Brisoys. *Grimod de la Reynière et son Groupe.* Paris: 1877.

Duclos, Charles P. *Memoires Secrets sur la Regne de Louis XIV*. Paris: Collin, 1808.

Ducros, Louis. *French Society in the 18th Century*. London: G. Bell, 1926.

Edwards, Matilda Betham. *Anglo-French Reminiscences, 1875–1899*. London: Chapman & Hall, 1900.

Forbes, James. *Letters from France*. London: 1806.

Furet, F., and Richet, D., *The French Revolution*. New York: Macmillan, 1970.

Goncourt, Edmond and Jules. *Histoire de la Société Francaise pendant le Directoire*. Paris: G. Charpentier, 1892.

Goncourt, Edmond and Jules. *The Goncourt Journals*. Paris: E. Fasquelle, 1891.

Goodrich, Frank Boott. *The Court of Napoleon*. New York: Derby and Jackson, 1857.

Le Grand d'Aussy. *Histoire de la Vie Privée à la Française*. Paris: 1782.

Gronow, Captain Rees Howell. *Reminiscences and Recollections, 1810–1860*. London: Smith, Elder, 1865 and 1866.

Guedalla, Philip. *The Second Empire*. London: Hodder, 1937.

Herbodeaux, Eugene; and Thalamus, Paul. *Georges Auguste Escoffier*. London: Practical Press Ltd., 1955.

Heritier, Jean. *Catherine de Medicis*. Paris: Fayard, 1942.

Hugon, Cecile. *Social France in the 17th Century*. New York: Macmillan, 1911.

Huddleston, Sisley. *Paris Salons, Cafes, Studios*. Philadelphia: Lippincott, 1928.

Jackson, Catherine, Lady. *Old Paris*. Boston: J. Knight Co., 1895.

Jackson, Catherine, Lady. *The Old Regime*. Boston: J. Knight Co., 1896.

Jarvis, James J. *Parisian Sights and French Principles*. New York: Harper Bros., 1855.

Lamothe-Langon, Etienne L., Baron de, *Evenings with Prince Cambacérès*. Philadelphia: Carey & Hart, 1838.

Lecestre, Leon. *Memoires de Gourville*. Paris: Historical Society of France, 1895.

Levron, Jacques. *Daily Life at Versailles in the 17th Century.* New York: Macmillan, 1968.

Mercier, Jean Sebastien. *Tableau de Paris.* Amsterdam: 1783.

Neville, R. *The World of Fashion.* London: Methuen & Co., 1923.

Newnham-Davis, Lieutenant-Colonel N. *Dinners and Diners.* London: 1899.

Palatine, Charlotte Elizabeth, Princess. *Letters of Madame.* New York: Appleton, 1925.

Potocka, Anna, Countess. *Memoires.* Paris: Plon-Nourritt, 1902.

Ritz, Marie. *César Ritz, Host to the World.* Philadelphia and New York: Lippincott, 1938.

Robiquet, Jean. *La Vie Quotidienne au Temps de Napoleon.* Paris: Hachette, 1944.

Saint-Simon, Louis de Rouvroy, Duc de. *Memoires.* Paris: Hachette, 1901.

Sala, George. *Paris is Herself Again.* London: 1880.

Vizetelly, Ernest Alfred. *Republican France.* London: Tinsley, 1873.

Vizetelly, Ernest Alfred. *Court Life of the Second Empire.* New York: Scribner's, 1907.

Whitehurst, Felix. *Court and Social Life in France.* London: Tinsley, 1873.

Young, Arthur. *Travels in France.* London: Bell, 1892.

All cookbooks and works on gastronomy cited in the text, such as those by La Varenne, Marin, Menon, Grimod de la Reynière, Carême, Dubois, Escoffier (1902), etc., are from the private collection of Esther B. Aresty.

Index

Note: Page numbers in *italics* refer to illustrations. Page numbers in **boldface** refer to recipes.